AF378287

Tom Murphy

17 APR 87
BARROW -IN·FURNESS
CUMBRIA
LA14 2QY.

# KLIMT

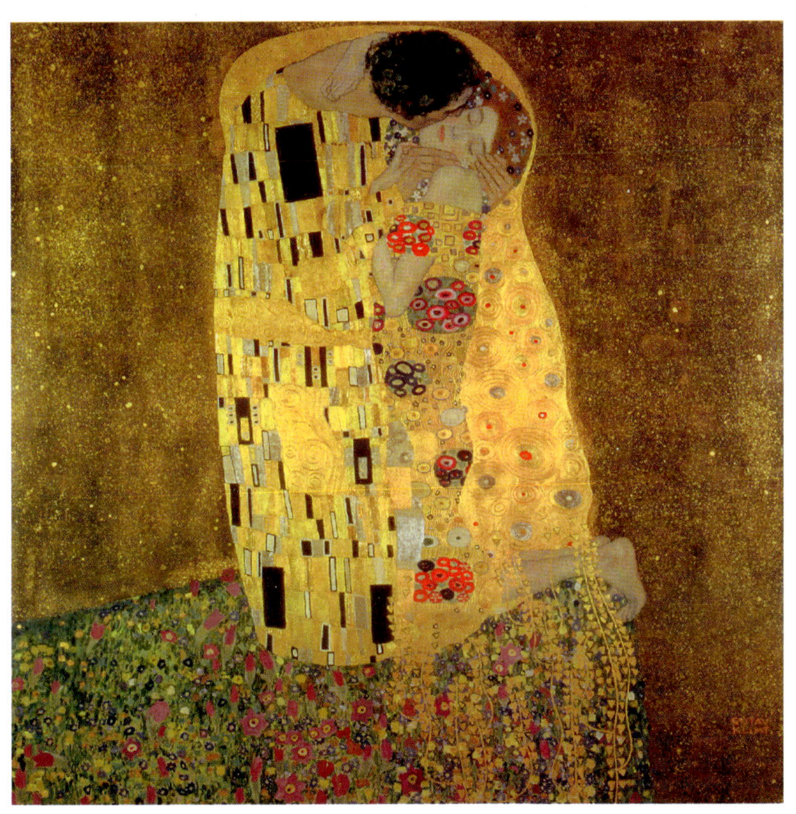

Published by Pulteney Press
1 Riverside Court
St Johns Road
Bath BA2 6PD



ISBN 978-1-906734-66-4

1 3 5 7 9 10 8 6 4 2



Designed and produced by Omnipress Limited, UK

Printed in Indonesia

Images were kindly supplied by Bridgeman Art Library, Getty Images and akg-images

# KLIMT

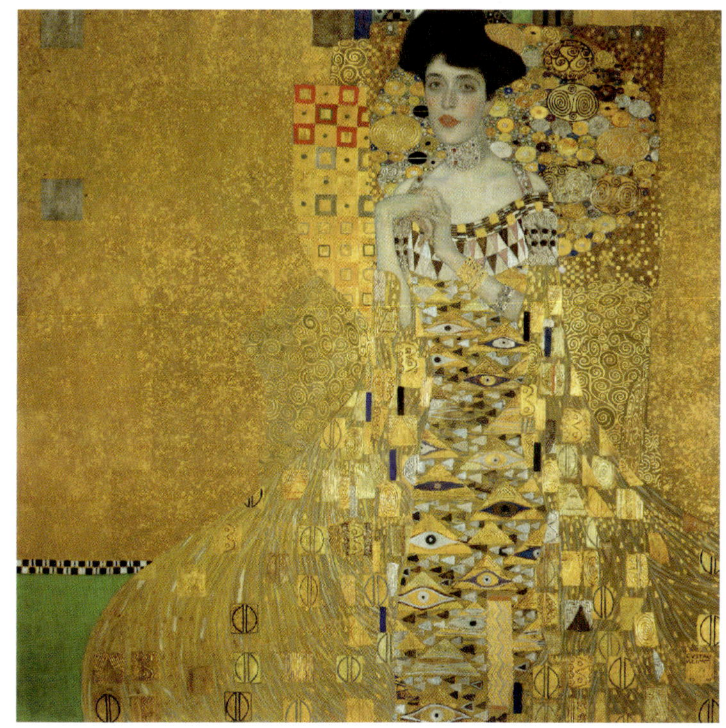

JANICE ANDERSON

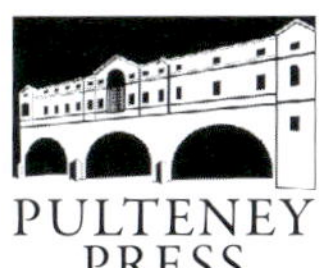

PULTENEY PRESS

# Contents

CONTENTS

# INTRODUCTION

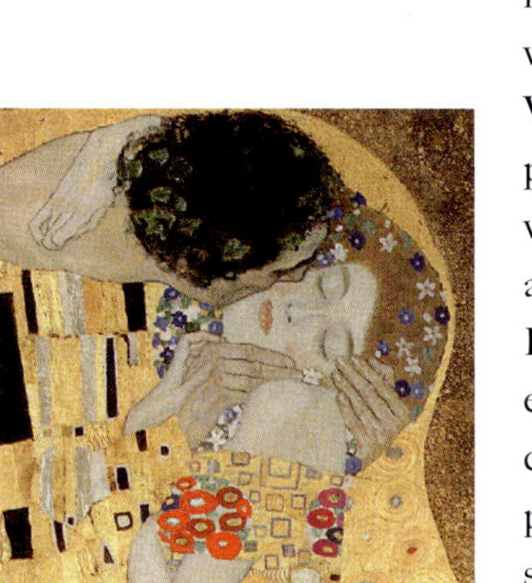

**THE KISS** *(Detail)*
*1907–8. Oil on canvas. 180 x 180 cm*
*Österreichische Galerie Belvedere,*
*Vienna.*

Gustav Klimt, who was born in Austria nearly a century and a half ago, painted pictures that have become among the most iconic images of our time. Countless copies of *The Kiss* (1907–8) hang on young people's walls all over the world, while it and Klimt's equally iconic *Judith I* (1901) attract thousands of visitors a year to the Belvedere Gallery in Vienna. Whether allegorical paintings, portraits – most of them of very beautiful women – decorative schemes for the walls and ceilings of buildings, or landscapes, Klimt's paintings are richly, even extravagantly decorative. As more than one critic has noted, in some of Klimt's paintings, the decoration, rather than the subject, is the real content of the work.

Klimt was born in Baumgarten, near Vienna, in Austria, on 14 July 1862. He was the eldest son in a family of seven born to an engraver, Ernst Klimt and his Viennese wife, Anna. Gustav and his younger brothers, Ernst and Georg, showed early strong artistic talent and all joined the School of Applied Art at the Royal and Imperial Museum for Art and Industry in Vienna in their early teens. Ernst became a painter and Georg, choosing the path of sculptor and engraver, made many of the frames for Gustav's paintings, so designed that they became an essential part of the complete work. At the School of Applied Art the teaching was geared to art as a practical craft, rather than a fine art, and was still very academic in the 1870s, the ferment of artistic change being felt throughout the Austro-Hungarian Empire in the second half of the nineteenth century having not yet made much of a mark there.

Gustav Klimt showed considerable promise from the outset, and was given several commissions while still a student at the School. One of the most publicly notable of these early commissions, carried out with his brother Ernst and a fellow student, Franz Matsch, was the provision of the artwork designs for the procession that the Viennese entrepreneur and painter, Hans Makart, organised as the highlight of the Silver Wedding celebrations of the Emperor Franz Josef and the Empress Elisabeth in

1879. Klimt finished his training at the School of Applied Arts in 1883. Almost at once he set up his own studio, with Ernst and Franz Matsch, and formed the Artists' Company with them.

While Klimt's training may have been academic, he had still absorbed much of the new thinking and attitudes that were causing so many changes in the European art scene at the time. With Vienna at the cross-roads between Western Europe and the East, there was much for a young artist to absorb. Klimt was drawn early to the avant-garde in European art, and drew inspiration from Impressionism, Symbolism and the great decorative style, Art Nouveau, which in Austria was called *Jugendstil*. Art Nouveau, a conscious rejection of the academic 'historicism' of much nineteenth-century European art, had as one of its main intellectual threads the English Arts and Crafts movement and in its most characteristic form used the sinuous curves and asymmetrical lines of plants. Art Nouveau was a major decorative style in Western Europe and the United States from the early 1890s until the First World War.

For a young artist in Vienna there were many other influences as well. Klimt's work, over his lifetime, showed him drawing on

such exotic sources as Byzantine art (particularly as it was displayed in the Byzantine mosaics in the churches of Ravenna), Mycenian metalwork (perhaps because of his Bohemia-born father's work as a metal, especially gold, engraver), Persian miniature painting and rug-making, and Japanese prints and screens (an important influence on the Impressionists).

The earliest work taken on by the three young artists of the Artist's Company continued along the lines of their School-time commissions and included designs for the interior of a municipal theatre in Fiume. At the same time, Klimt was also doing conventional easel painting, completing such romantic works as *Fable* (1883) and *Idyll* (1884). Both these paintings developed from painted sketches Klimt did as illustrations for a book called *Allegorien und Embleme*. Then in 1887 came Klimt's first big artistic, rather than decorative, commission. The Artists' Company had been working for a year on painting decorations on the two splendid staircases of the new Burgtheater being built, with many other grand buildings, on Vienna's magnificent new Ringstrasse. Klimt's contribution to the work included paintings of scenes with a theatrical theme, such as

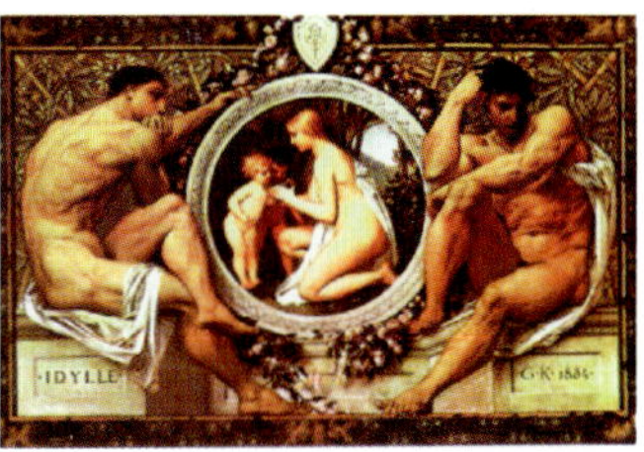

**IDYLL**
*Oil on canvas. 1884. 50 x 74 cm.*
*Historical Museum, Vienna.*

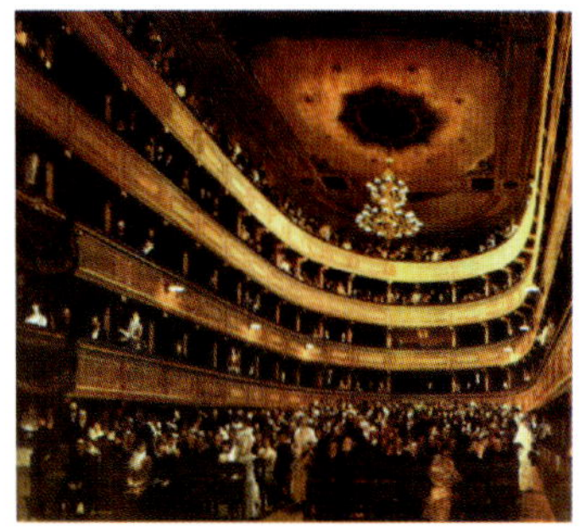

**AUDITORIUM OF THE OLD BURGTHEATER**
*1888. Gouache on paper. 82 x 92 cm. Historisches Museum der Stadt Wien, Vienna.*

'The Altar of Dionysus' and 'Shakespeare's Globe Theatre'.

Now Klimt was asked by Vienna's city council to paint an interior view, complete with an audience of Vienna's high society, of the old Burgtheater, which was soon to be pulled down. Klimt's gouache painting, *Auditorium of the Old Burgtheater* (1888), done in a classic, almost photographic, style much appreciated by the theatre's wealthy middle-class patrons, won him the newly created Imperial Award in 1890, two years after he and Franz Matsch had been given Golden Crosses of Merit for their work on the new Burgtheater. The painting also brought him to the attention of the leading figures in Viennese high society, including the Emperor himself.

Klimt was not, himself, very appreciative of his *Auditorium* painting, thinking it old-fashioned and too tied to traditional art forms. He chose to turn his back on his new-found success and went travelling in Europe for the next two years, visiting places as far apart as Cracow in Poland and Venice in Italy. He did not go to Paris, the centre of European avant-garde art in the late 1880s.

Back in Vienna in 1890, Klimt seemed to take up pretty much where he had left off two years before, beginning work on

designing decorations for the spandrels and intercolumnar spaces on the grand staircase in Vienna's Museum of Art History. Hans Makart had done much of the preliminary design work and also much of the finished work in the Museum before his death in 1884. Although Klimt found the traditionally-based specifications for the work inhibiting, he still managed to introduce new elements into his designs. In the spandrels for which he was asked to provide 'Egyptian Art' and 'Greek Antiquity' themes, for instance, his female figures were stylized and strongly symbolic.

Once again, Klimt's work found favour, and in 1891 he, his brother Ernst, and Franz Matsch all received the 'highest possible recognition' for their work on the Museum of Art History decorations. In this year, Klimt joined the Co-operative Society of Austria and it was even whispered that, although not yet 30, he might be awarded a professorship at the Academy.

No professorship was forthcoming, however, and the year in which he turned 30 was marked by something much sadder – the deaths of his brother Ernst and of his father. From this time, a darker tone came into Klimt's art. After Ernst's death, his beautiful wife, Emilie Flöge, became Gustav

Klimt's close companion, life-long friend and the subject of one of his finest portraits. Once again, Klimt went travelling, this time to Hungary, where he fulfilled a theatre-decorating commission for Prince Esterhazy in 1893. Back in Vienna in 1894, Klimt was soon hard at work on a second portfolio of 'Allegory and Emblem' pictures, out of which developed such archetypal Klimt paintings as *Love* (1895), with its marked allegorical symbolism.

In 1894, the Austrian Ministry of Education commissioned Klimt and Matsch to provide paintings for another great institution, Vienna University. This major commission involved designing a series of Faculty Paintings for the ceiling of the university's Grand Auditorium. It was this commission that finally caused Klimt to break with the traditional and academic Austrian art establishment.

Klimt's great Faculty Paintings murals for the University, preceded as they were by many preliminary drawings, sketches and studies which have themselves become sought-after works of art, had as their subjects *Jurisprudence*, *Medicine* and *Philosophy*, all with the underlying theme of 'The Victory of Light over Darkness'. Klimt, by now far from traditional art teaching

along the road towards modernity in art, chose an approach that had little to do with academically rational science and much to do with a theatrically allegorical depiction of his three subjects.

Even his sketches aroused considerable hostility among the art and academic establishments in Vienna, and so long-lasting was the public controversy that the paintings were never hung in the University. Klimt eventually returned the advance commission he had been paid by the state. One painting, *Medicine*, first shown publicly in 1901, when it was severely criticised in the press, ended up in the Austrian Gallery in Vienna. The Faculty Paintings were forcibly removed from their Jewish owners by the Nazis in the 1930s and taken to Schloss Immendorf in Lower Austria, where they were destroyed when Schloss Immendorf was burned down during the Allied advance in 1945. Many other paintings by Klimt that had also been taken to Schloss Immendorf were burnt in 1945, including two fine murals, *Music II* (1898) and *Schubert at the Piano* (1899) that Klimt did for the Music Room of the Nikolaus Dumba Palace in Vienna.

In 1897, when the Faculty Paintings controversy was raging, Klimt left the

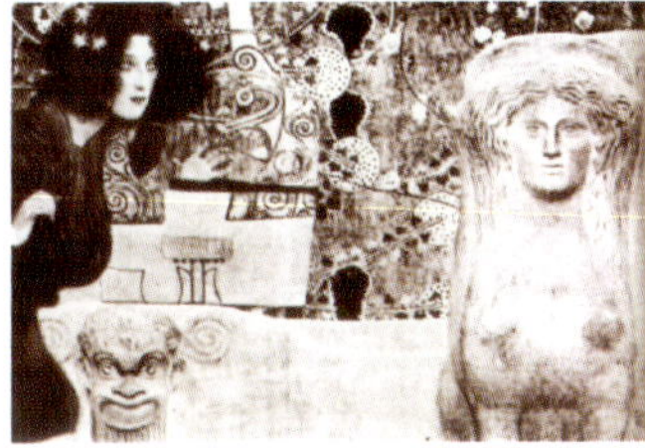

**MUSIC II**
*1898. Oil on canvas. 150 x 200 cm. This painting was destroyed by fire at Immendorf Castle in 1945.*

Co-operative Society of Austrian Artists and, with Joseph Maria Olbrich and the architect Josef Hoffmann, founded in Vienna a Secession group of artists, of which he was the first president. Such groups had already been founded in Germany, notably in Munich, by artists wanting to break away from the established art world in order to further the aims of the various modern movements in European art, especially Impressionism. In the Viennese Secession, interest in the English Arts and Crafts movement, with its emphasis on the style and function of the applied arts, was perhaps stronger than in other Secession groups because Josef Hoffmann, who was later to found the Viennese Workshop, felt as keen an interest in it as he did in the work of the Scottish architect Charles Rennie Mackintosh.

Within a year of the Viennese Secession's founding, the group had begun publishing a magazine, called *Ver Sacrum* (after an ancient Roman initiation rite), taken the goddess Pallas Athene as its main symbol and icon, and held its first exhibition in Vienna's Horticultural Rooms. The poster for this all-important first exhibition was designed by Klimt, who provided an allegorical theme: Theseus, protected by Pallas Athene, fighting the Minotaur. When the poster was also used as the cover of *Ver Sacrum*, some censoring was considered necessary, with Theseus's private parts being obscured by a tree, which Klimt added to the picture. As for the goddess herself, she was the subject of one of Klimt's most iconic paintings of the period, *Pallas Athene* (1898), in which the metal of the goddess's helmet and breastplate was echoed in the painting's metal Art Nouveau-style frame.

After its first exhibition, held early in 1898, the Viennese Secession exhibitions were held in its own Secession Building, designed in a very modern style by Joseph Maria Olbrich, who included a view of his Secession Building in his poster for the IInd Secession Exhibition, in November, 1898. Here, the artists of the Viennese Secession pursued their great aim of offering a 'purified, modern view of art', embracing not just art itself, but also architecture, the applied arts, including furniture and decorative objects, and fashion.

Klimt took a lively and informed interest in all these aspects of Secessionist art, with his greatest contributions outside his main field, painting, being the designs he did for

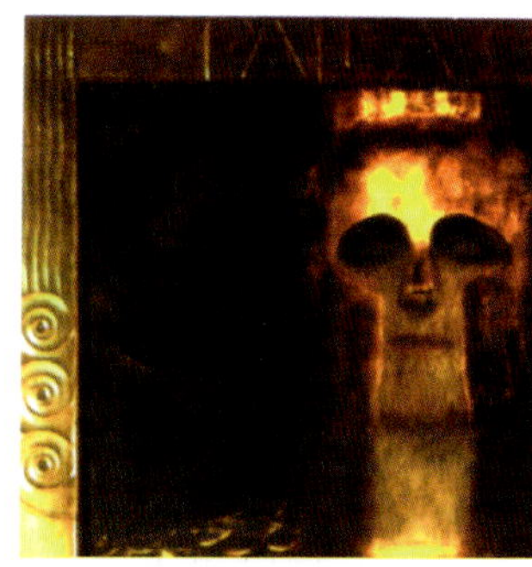

**PALLAS ATHENE**
*1898. Oil on canvas. 75 x 75 cm.*
*Historisches Museum der Stadt Wien,*
*Vienna.*

building interiors. These reached a peak of brilliance in the mosaic frieze he designed between 1905 and 1911 for the Dining Room of the great palace in Brussels designed by Klimt's Secession colleague, Josef Hoffmann, for a rich coal magnate, Adolphe Stoclet. Klimt chose the Tree of Life as his motif for the Palais Stoclet frieze, and executed it in a brilliantly designed Art Nouveau style.

The theme of the young male hero at the centre of a struggle for salvation – by analogy, a struggle between art and reality, between the younger and the older generations – depicted by Klimt on the Ist Secession Exhibition poster, was to recur in his work, notably in his stunning *Beethoven Frieze*, done for the XIVth Exhibition of the Viennese Secession in 1902. The frieze was designed for the walls of a room dominated by a statue of Beethoven by the sculptor Max Klinger.

Klimt took as his theme Beethoven's great Ninth Symphony with its 'Ode to Joy' final movement. While the climax of the frieze is a couple, framed in golden patterning, embracing and sending 'a kiss to the whole world', one of its most arresting sections, 'A Yearning for Happiness', features a Golden Knight – symbol of heroism and representing the spirit of the Secession

movement. The model for the Golden Knight is said to have been the composer Gustav Mahler, whose music Klimt greatly admired. Some five years later, the climactic kiss of the Beethoven Frieze had become *The Kiss* (1907-8), a wonderfully tender yet erotic painting that marked the climax of Klimt's 'golden period'.

By this time, Klimt had widened his depiction of the 'young male hero' theme. For some time, his depiction of the female form had been moving far from his early, conventional portrayals of women. Now, Klimt was painting the female figure in near-heroic style. One picture, *Nuda Veritas* (1899) highlights the change. Shown first in a black chalk drawing in *Ver Sacrum*, the final painting of a seductive and erotic nude woman, done in an Impressionistic style, uncompromisingly conveyed Klimt's view of art as a clearing away of the old, stagnant approach to life and art and a concentration on truth. As the inscription above the figure in the chalk drawing said, 'Truth is Fire. Truth Means Illumination and Burning'.

1897, the year in which the Vienna Secession was founded, turned out to be something of a watershed year for Klimt, for this was the year in which he began seriously to paint landscapes. From the outset, his

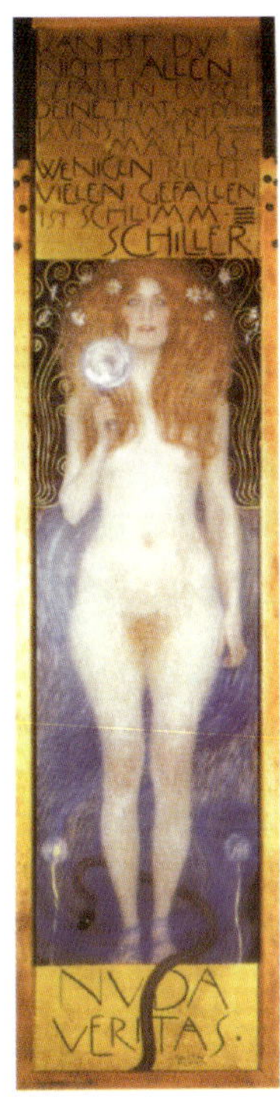

**NUDA VERITAS**
*1899. Oil on canvas. 252 x 56.2 cm. Österreichische Nationalbibliothek, Vienna.*

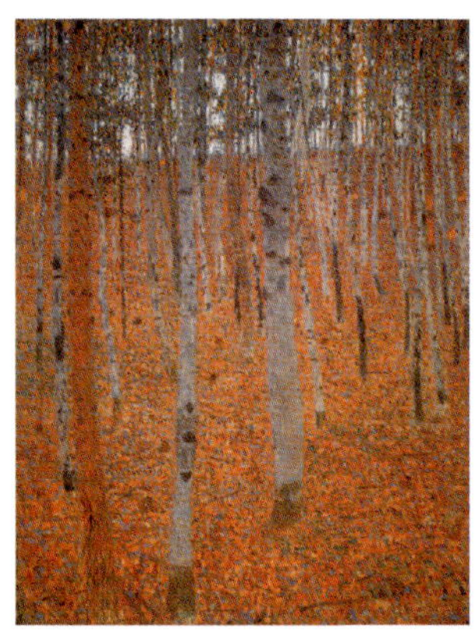

**BEECH FOREST**
*1900. Oil on card.*

approach to landscape painting was unusual. Rejecting the horizontal, rectangular format favoured by most landscape painters, Klimt almost invariably painted his landscapes on square canvases. Unlike his increasingly decorative and stylised portraits of women, which he began painting in earnest in the first decade of the twentieth century, Klimt's landscapes owed much more to the techniques of the Impressionists. Here were the short brushstrokes of pure colour, applied with a certain restraint in such early landscapes as *Orchard* (1898) and *Farmhouse with Birch Trees* (1900), but set on later canvases, such as *The Pear Tree* (1903) and *Poppy Field* (1907) as precisely and dramatically as in the paintings of the Pointillistes. Here, too, were the open compositions with large, relatively empty foregrounds so often seen in the paintings of Monet.

Klimt's landscapes tend to come as a surprise, even a revelation, to people encountering his work in galleries and exhibitions for the first time, for Klimt has become known as a painter of the female form. It is his portraits, rather than his landscapes, that define him in the public mind. It is perhaps not surprising that this should be so, for Klimt's portraits of women are unique in their decorative quality and their exoticism, while his increasingly extravagant use of gold leaf, rich colours, patterns and motifs turn his portraits into highly desirable jewels of art.

One such jewel, Klimt's first portrait, done in 1907, of *Adele Bloch-Bauer*, wife of a rich industrialist and believed to have been Klimt's mistress, caused a sensation when it was sold in New York in 2006 for $135 million. *Adele Bloch-Bauer I* is a stunning icon of female beauty. Her pale, intelligent face is set on a long, jewel-collared neck arising from ivory sloping shoulders, and her slim hands are clasped high in front of her bosom. These are the only parts of her body depicted naturally. All else disappears in swirls and undulating curves of sumptuous patterns and motifs, all richly overlaid with gold.

While *Adele Bloch-Bauer I* stands at the pinnacle of Klimt's 'gold style', many others of his portraits of women come near to it in their decorative beauty. Even in his more relatively conventional portraits – *Portrait of Fritza Riedler* (1900), *Portrait of Margaret Stonborough-Wittgenstein* (1905), or *Portrait of Hermine Gallia* (1904), for instance – his use of colour and pattern is uniquely Klimt. As his unfinished *Portrait of a Lady* (1917–18) makes clear, Klimt planned his decorative portraits carefully, firmly stating the head from the start, and painting it quite naturally, while leaving the drawing of the body tentative, so that he had could alter shapes and patterns as the finished picture emerged. This is clearly the approach he took with such portraits as his magnificent full-length study of *Emilie Flöger* (1902), *Adele Bloch-Bauer II* (1912) and *Portrait of Eugenia Primavesi* (1913-14).

He used the same approach in other paintings of women – and there were many of them for Klimt was greatly attracted to women and to female beauty. His painting *Judith I* (1901) impresses everyone who sees it as an archetypal image of the femme fatale, a label which could also be attached to *Salome* (also known as *Judith II*) of 1901.

The female body provided Klimt with the material for paintings that were allegorical, symbolic, iconic and even mythological. Their composition was often very daring. There is, for instance, the circular shape of the body of *Danaë* (1907-8) – daring enough as a subject, anyway, since the myth tells the story of how Zeus entered Danaë in the shape of a shower of gold coins. Then there is the tenderly drawn, yet shockingly prominent shape of the pregnant nude woman who is the subject of *Hope I* (1903).

By the time Klimt came to paint *Hope II* (1907–8), the pregnancy of the female figure is hidden under a swelling, curved shape filled with swirling patterns.

In Klimt's later work, there is a hint of the harder edge of Expressionism, a style perhaps more suited to life in a Europe that was soon to be torn apart by the turmoil of the First World War. The woman depicted in *Salome*, for instance, seems harder, more rapacious than the figure in *Judith I*, while the later landscapes, most of them painted in the country round Lake Atter, where Klimt began spending his summers in 1900, or at Lake Garda in Italy, had also taken on the harder, darker lines characteristic of Expressionism.

Klimt, by now a revered figure in Austrian art, was a major influence on the early careers of several young artists, particularly Egon Schiele and Oskar Kokoschka, both of whom were his students and both of whom became leading Expressionist artists. But, even before he died, still in his 50s, in Vienna in February, 1918, Klimt's influence on the younger generation was waning, and it is unlikely that he would himself have abandoned his own distinctive style. Gustav Klimt's highly decorative style was both unique and inimitable.

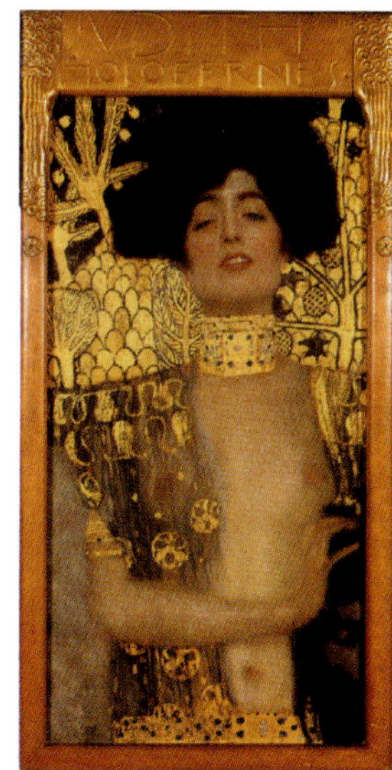

**JUDITH I**
*1901. Oil on canvas. 84 x 42 cm. Österreichische Galerie Belvedere, Vienna.*

# FABLE

*Oil on canvas. 1883. Historical Museum, Vienna.*
*84.5 x 117 cm.*

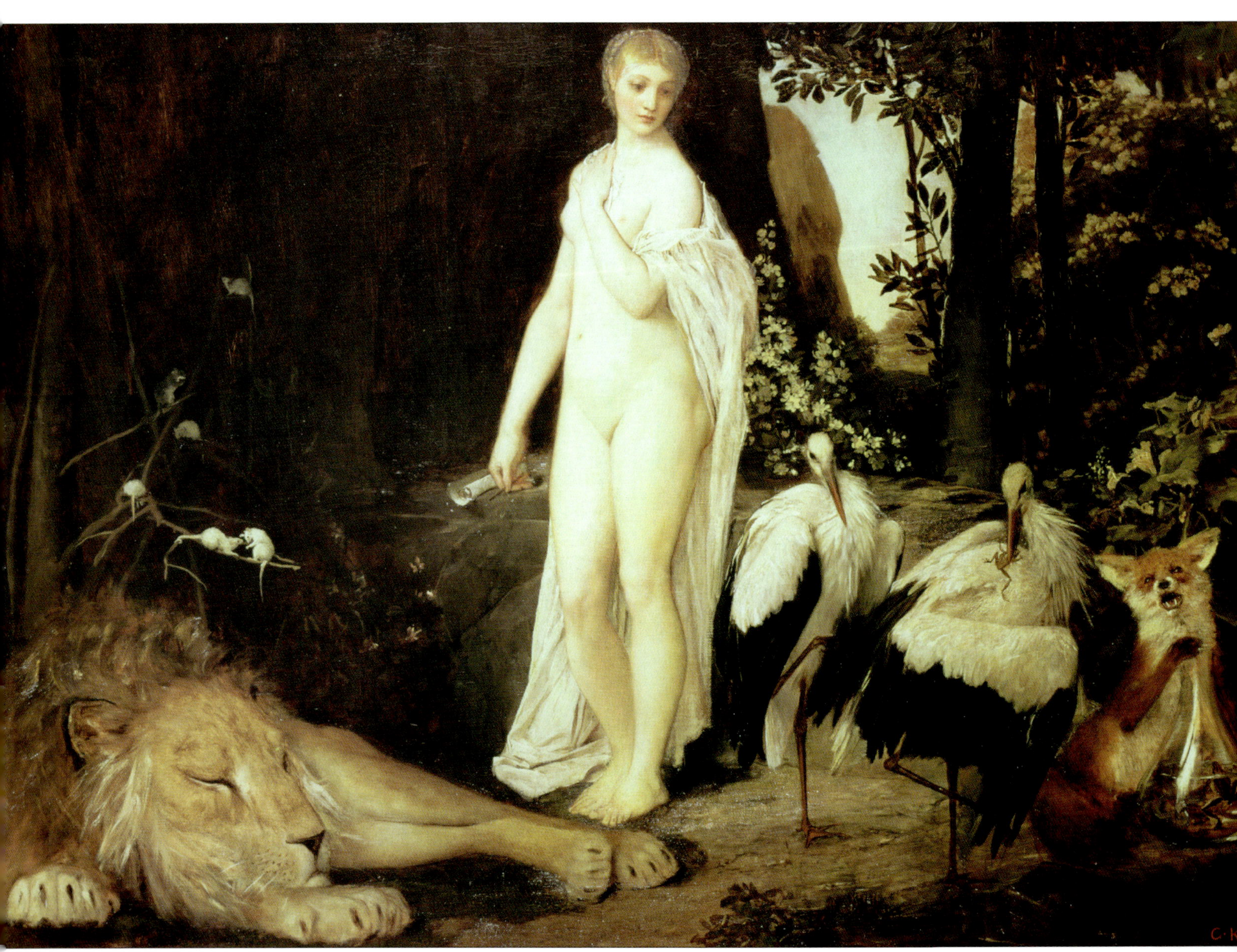

*Oil on canvas. 1884. Historisches Museum der Stadt Wien, Vienna, Austria.*
*50 x 74 cm.*

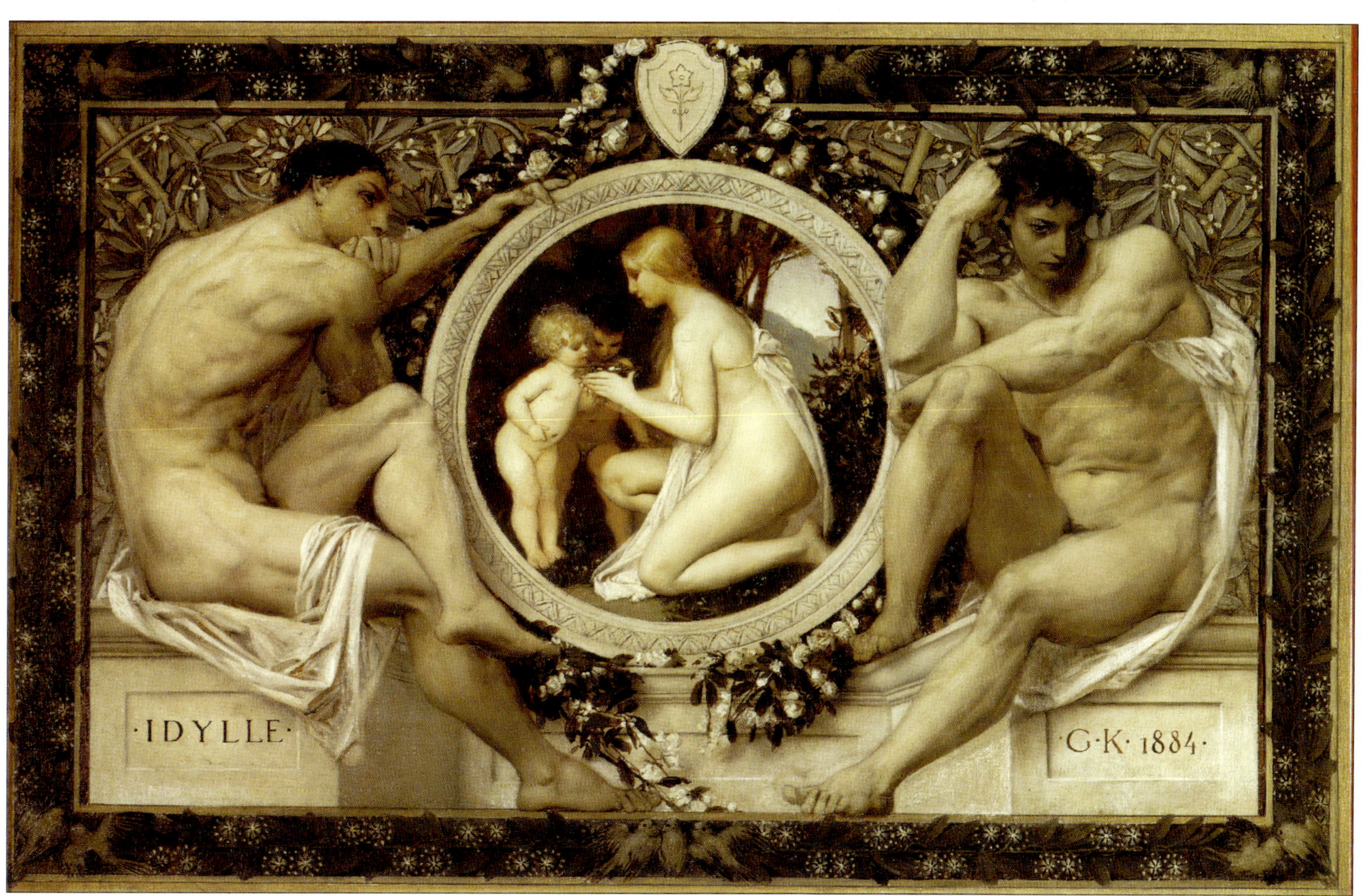

# DAS ANTIKE THEATER IN TAORMINA

*Oil/Stucco. 1887. Ceiling painting from the left staircase in the Burgtheatre, Vienna. 750 x 400 cm.*

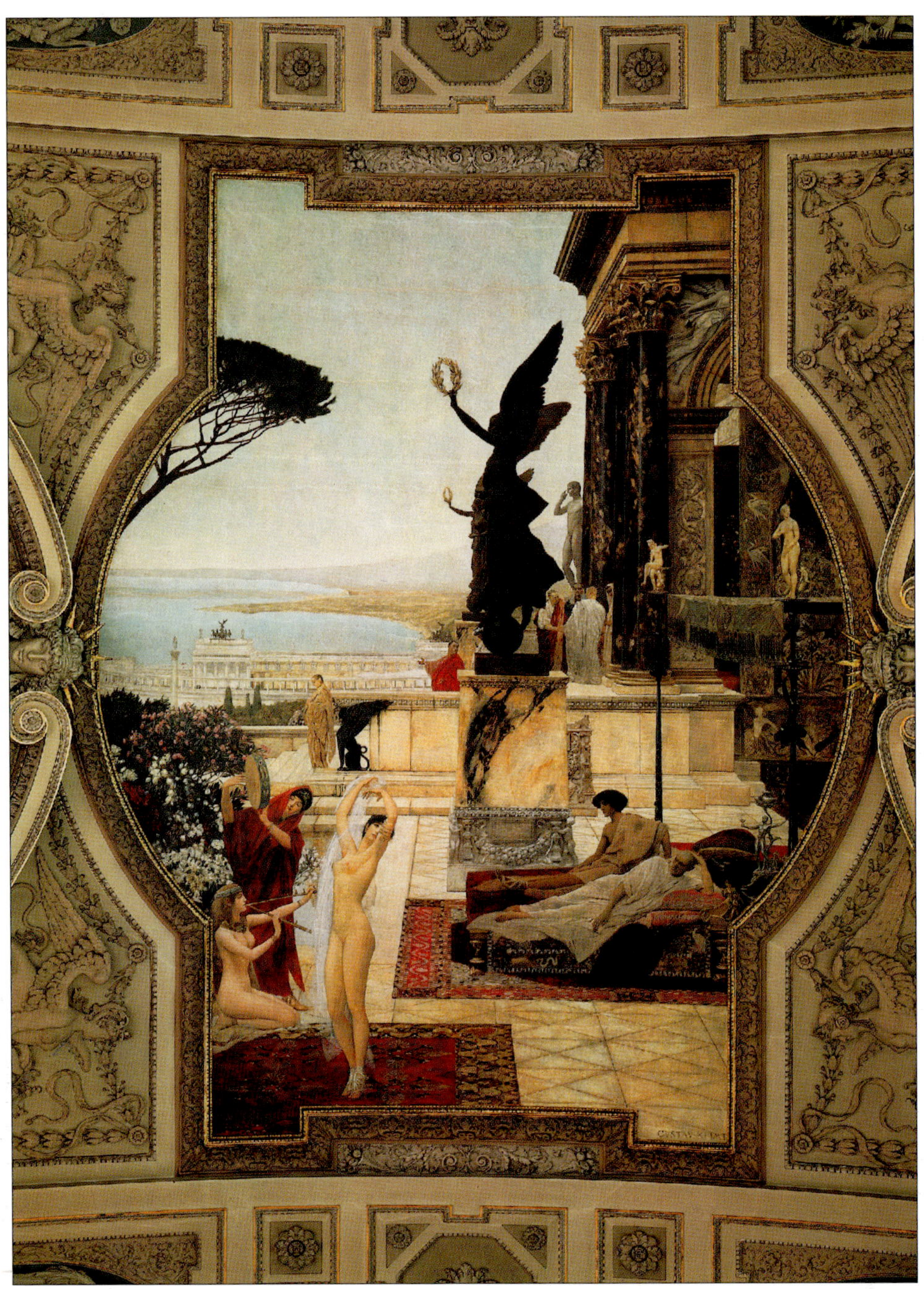

*Oil on canvas. 1888. Wien Museum Karlsplatz, Vienna, Austria.*
*82 x 92 cm.*

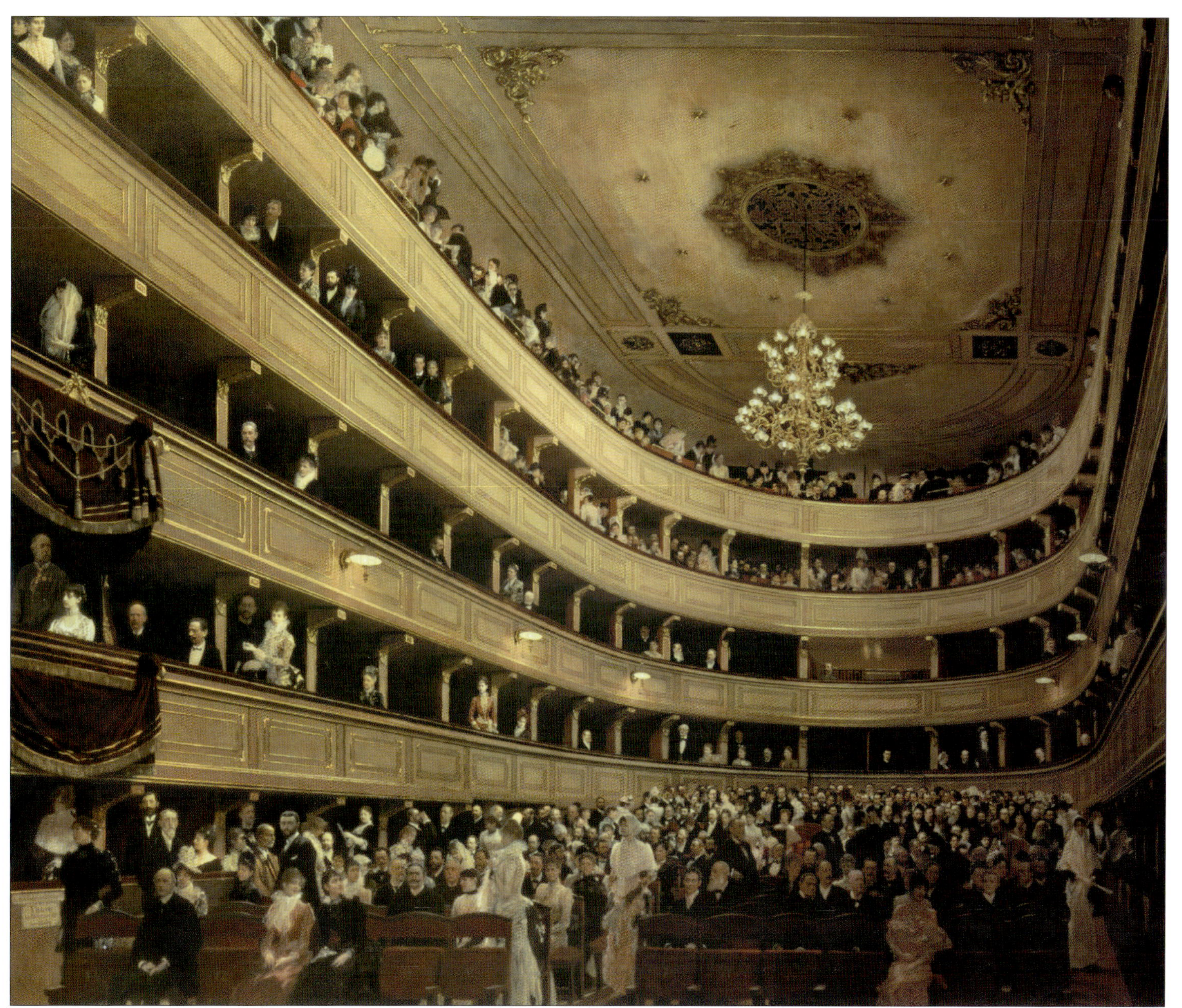

# THE PIANIST JOSEF PEMBAUER

*Oil on canvas. 1890. Tiroler Landesmuseum Ferdinandeum, Innsbruck.*
*69 x 55 cm.*

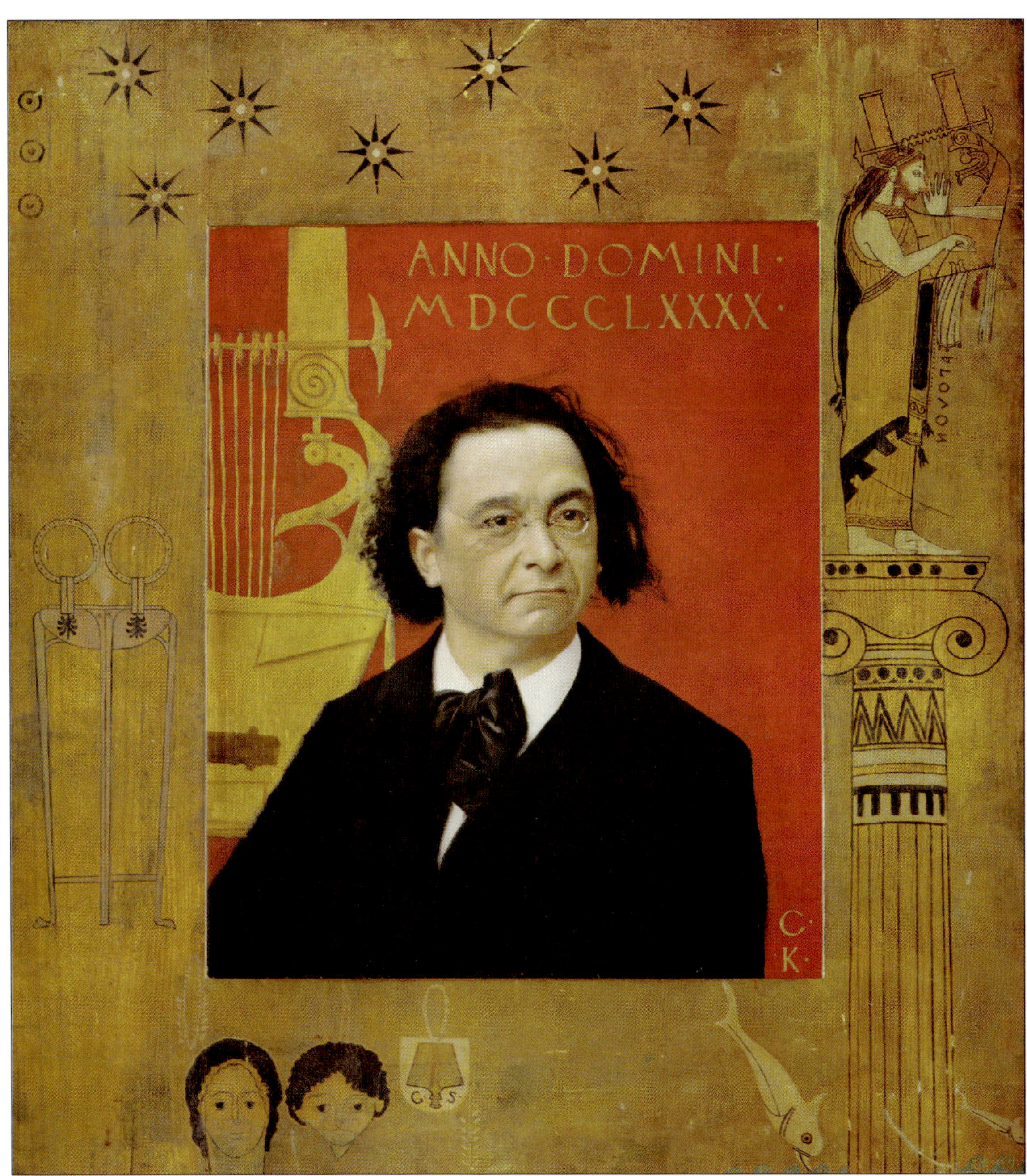

*Pastel on paper. 1891. Private collection. 67 x 41.5 cm.*

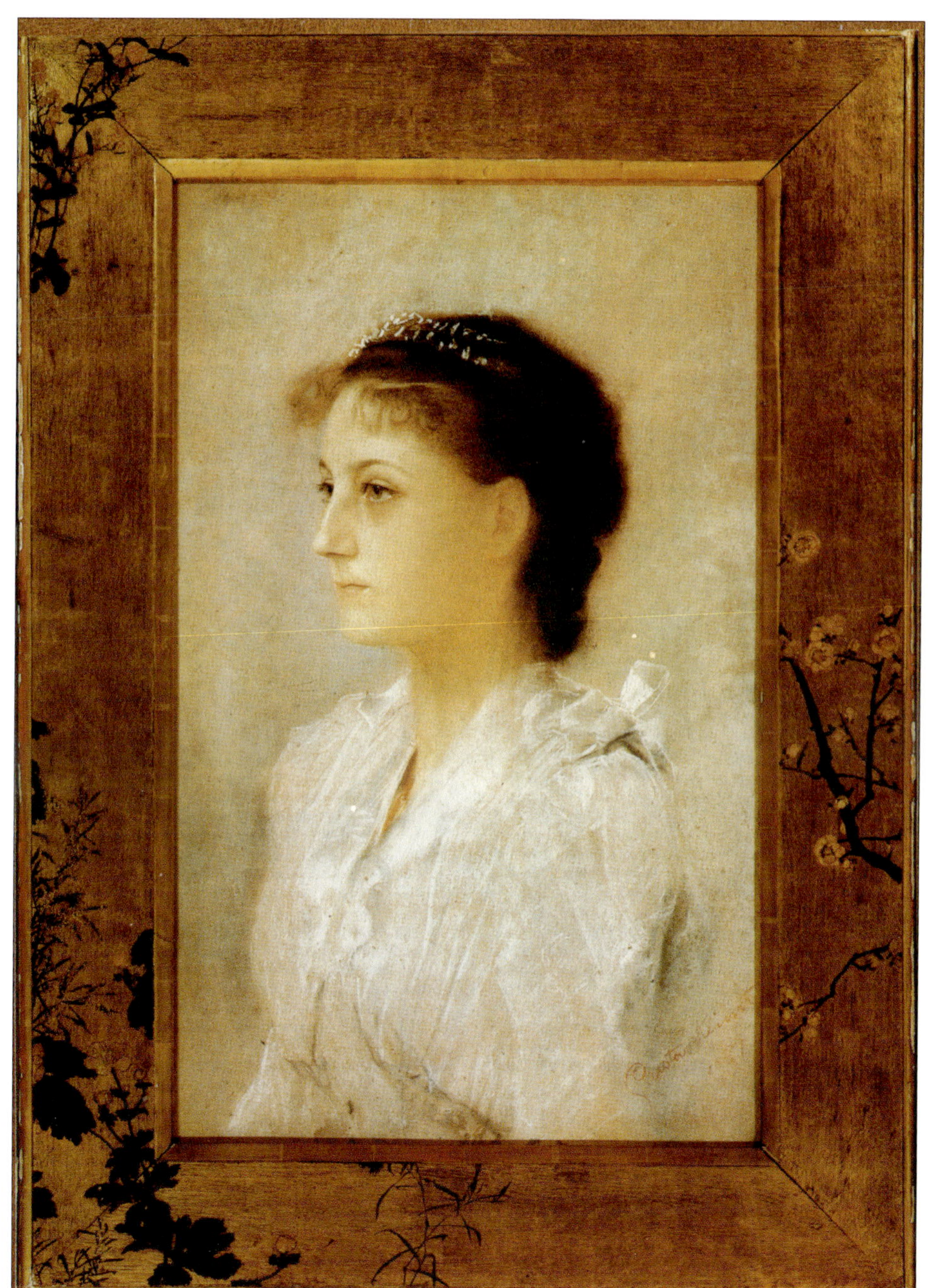

# PORTRAIT OF A LADY

*Oil on canvas. c19th century. Wien Museum Karlsplatz, Vienna, Austria.*
*39 x 23 cm.*

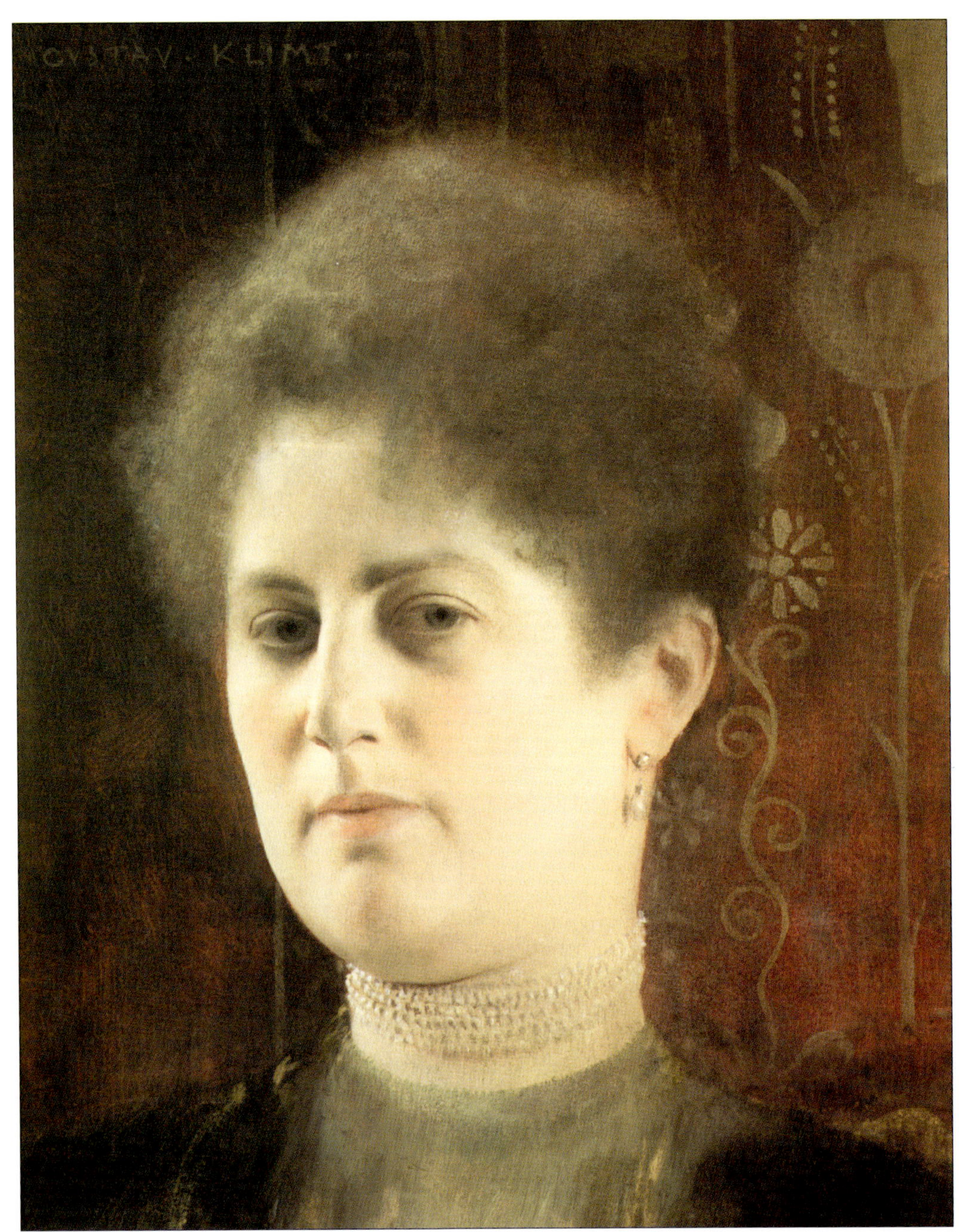

*Actor Josef Lewinsky (from 1858 Vienna Burgtheater). Oil on canvas. 1895.*
*Österreiche alerie im Belvedere, Vienna, Austria. 64 x 44 cm.*

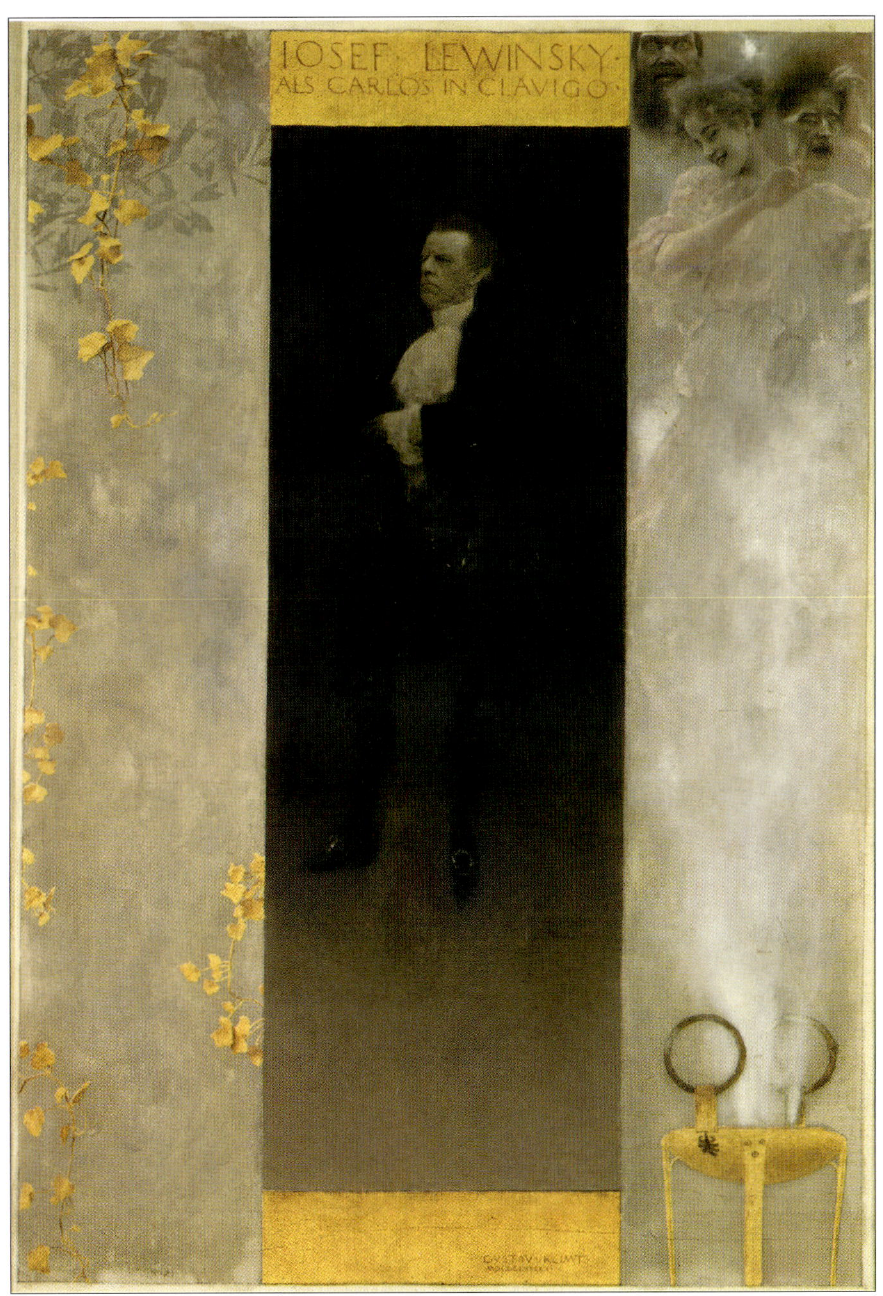

# LOVE

*Oil on canvas. 1895. Kunsthistorisches Museum, Vienna. Austria. 60 x 44 cm.*

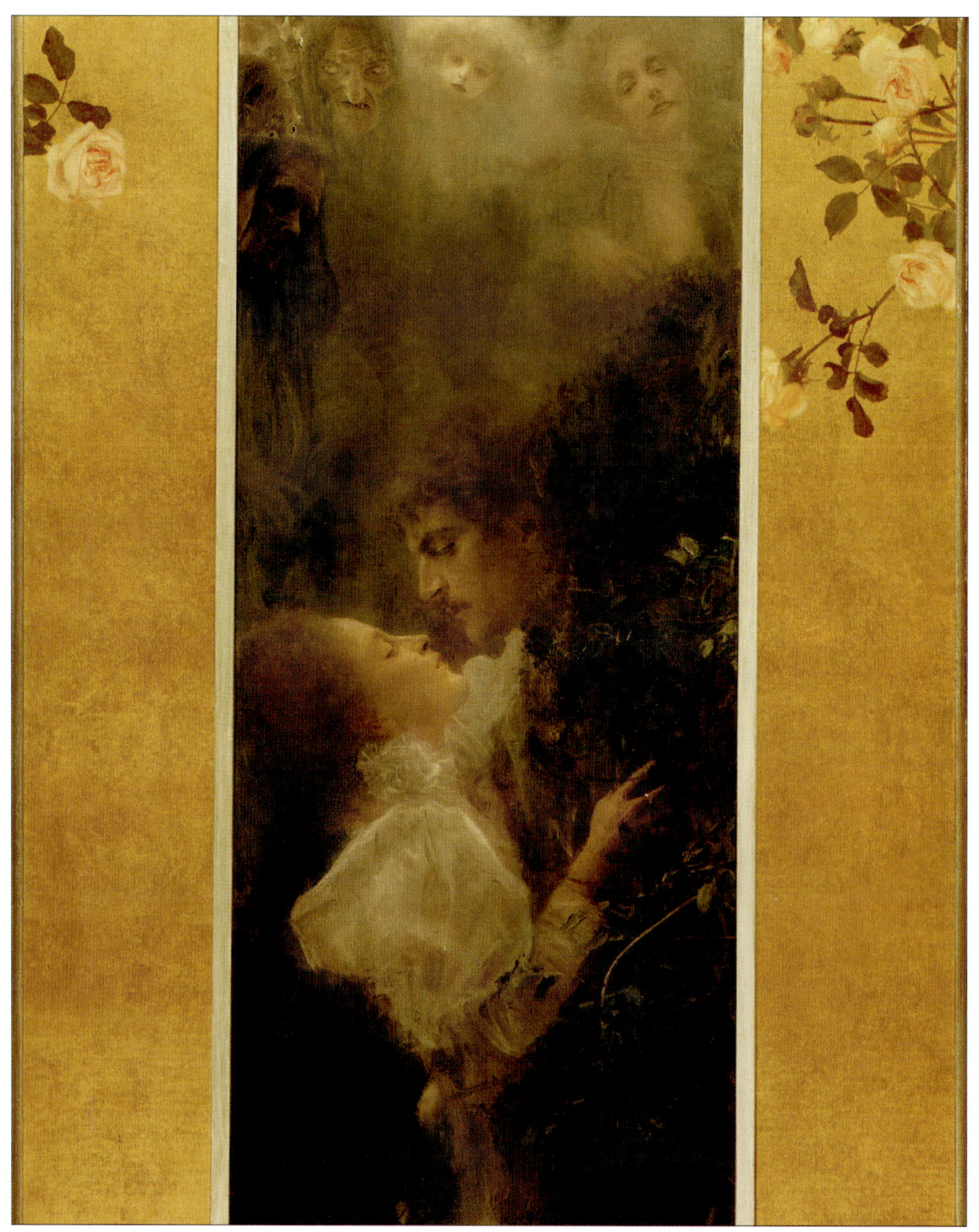

# TRAGEDY



*Drawing. 1897. Wien Museum Karlsplatz, Vienna, Austria. 42 x 31 cm.*

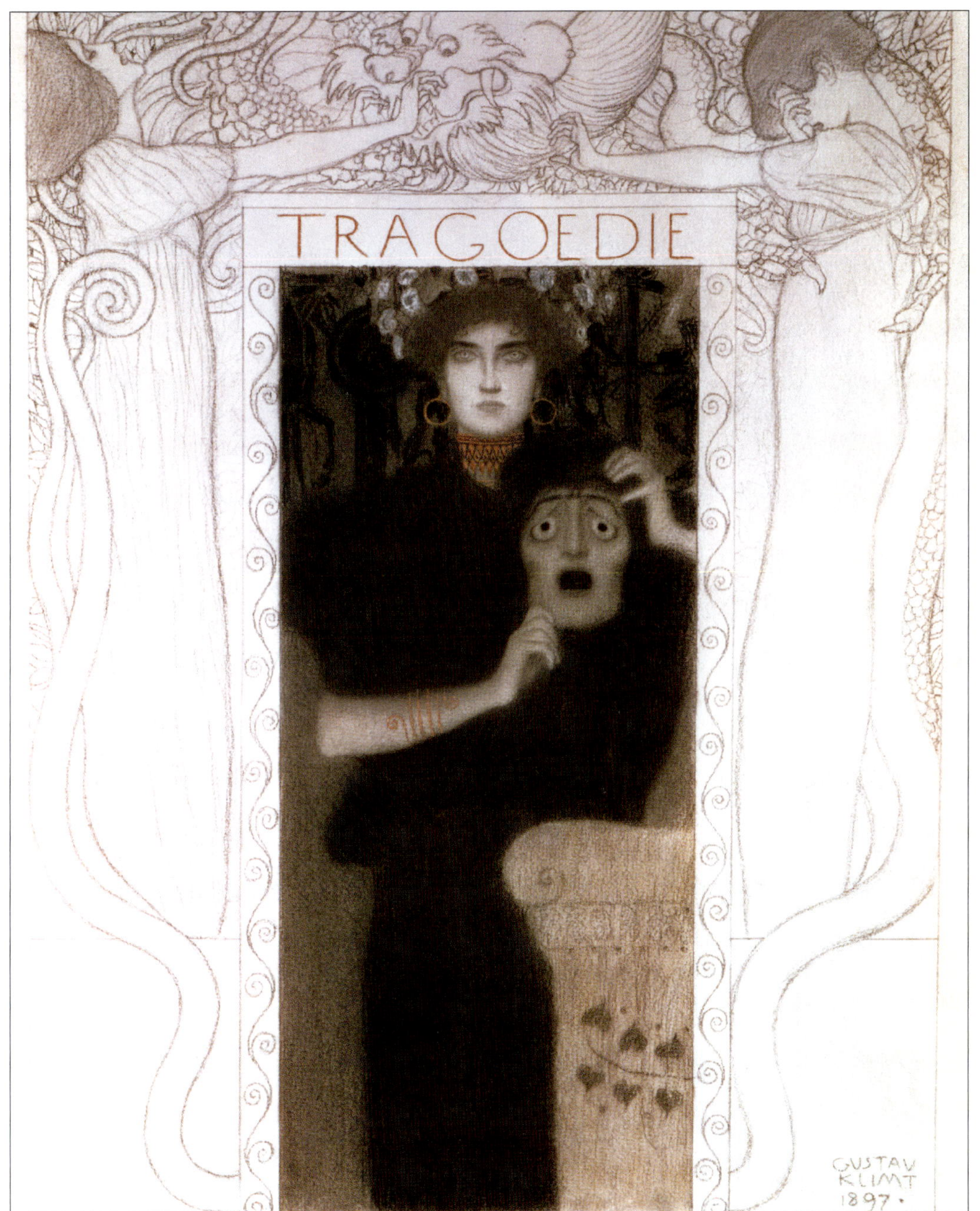

# PORTRAIT OF A LADY

*Pastel on paper. 1887–1907.*
*Allen Memorial Art Museum, Oberlin College, Ohio, USA. 51 x 28 cm.*

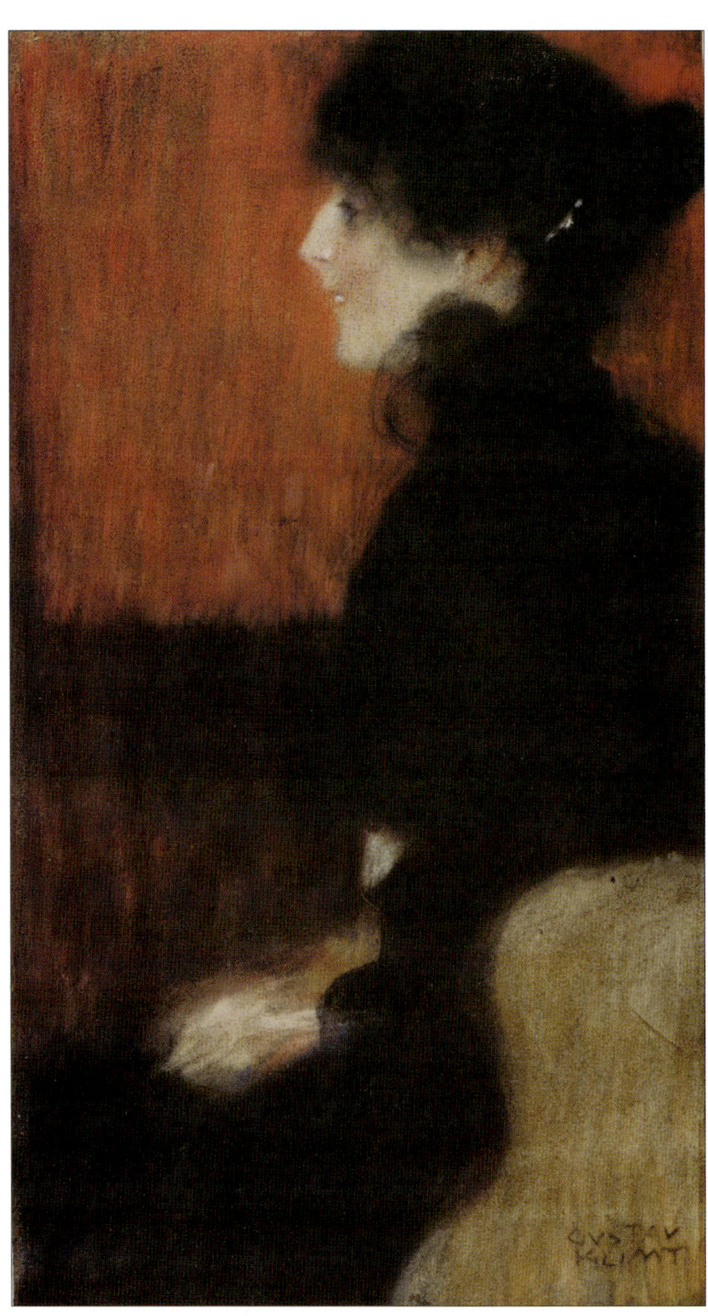

# THE BLOOD OF FISH


*Published in 'Ver Sacrum' magazine. Engraving. 1898. Private collection.*

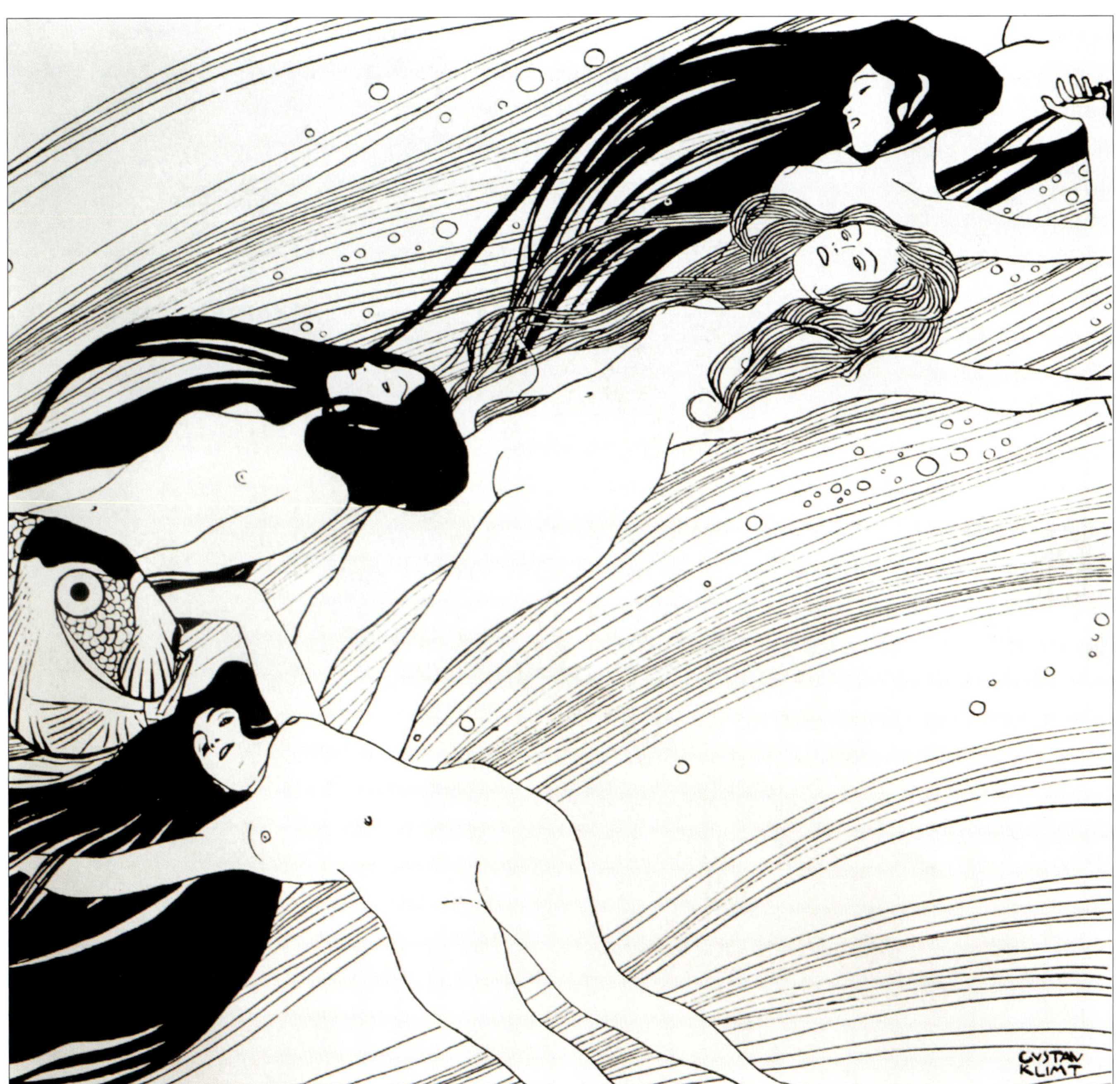

# PALLAS ATHENE

*Oil on canvas. 1898. Historical Museum, Vienna, Austria.*
*75 x 75 cm.*

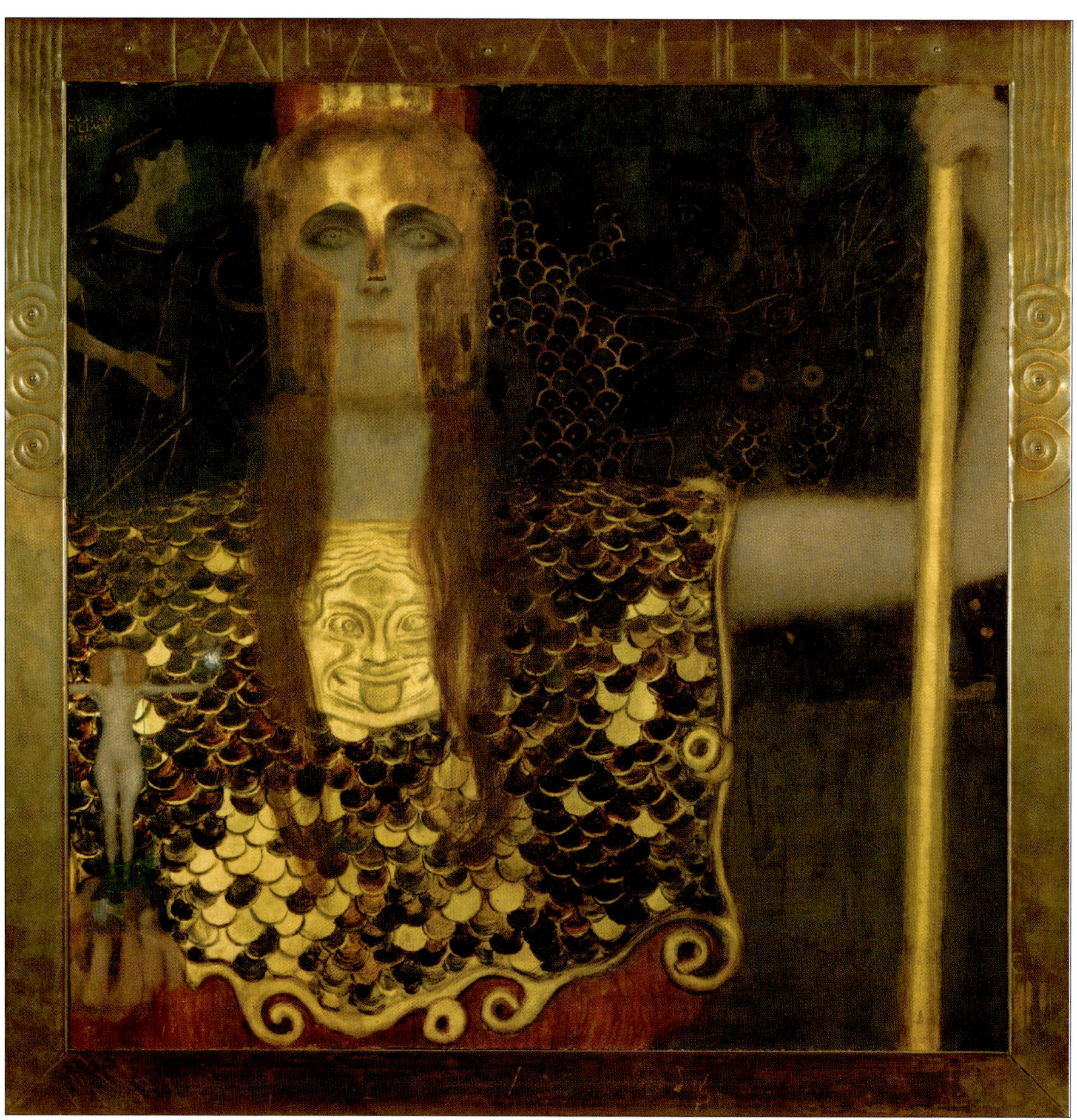

# PORTRAIT EN FACE

*Oil on canvas. 1898–99.*
*Österreiche Gallerie im Belvedere, Vienna, Austria. 45 x 34 cm.*

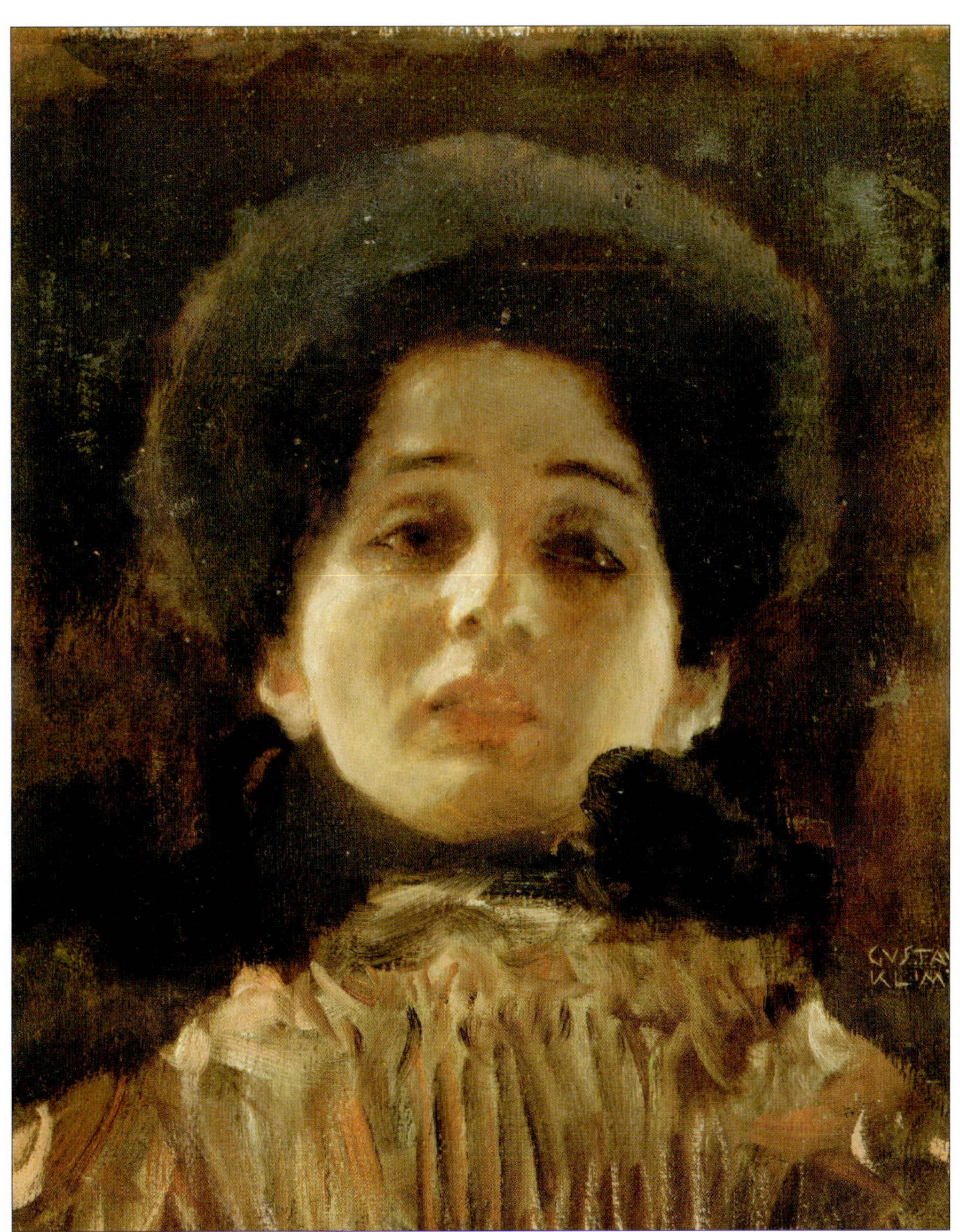

# SCHUBERT AT THE PIANO

*Oil on canvas. 1825. Destroyed by fire at Immendorf Castle in 1945.*
*150 x 200 cm.*

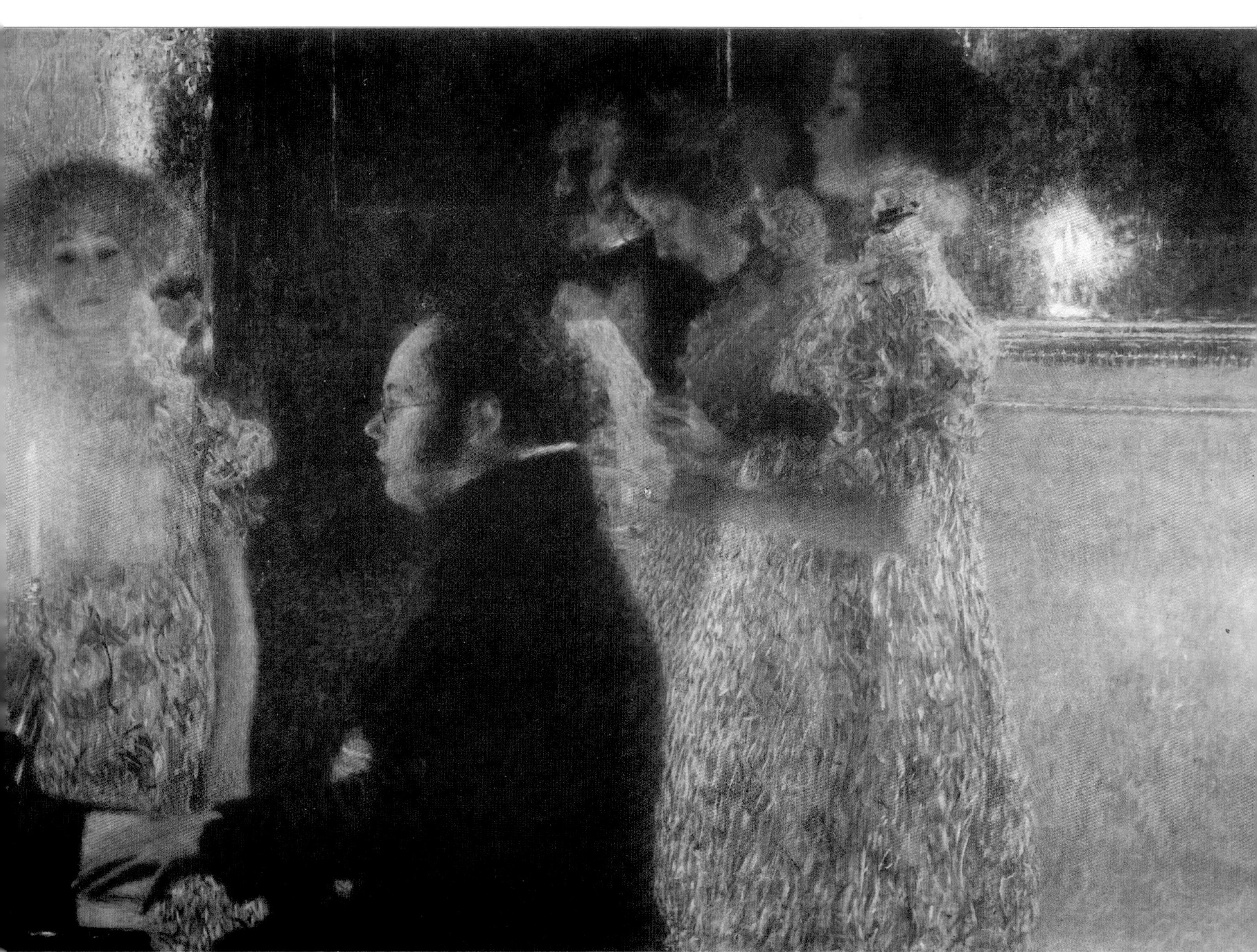

Oil on canvas. 1898. Osterreichische Galerie Belvedere, Vienna, Austria.
145 x 145 cm.

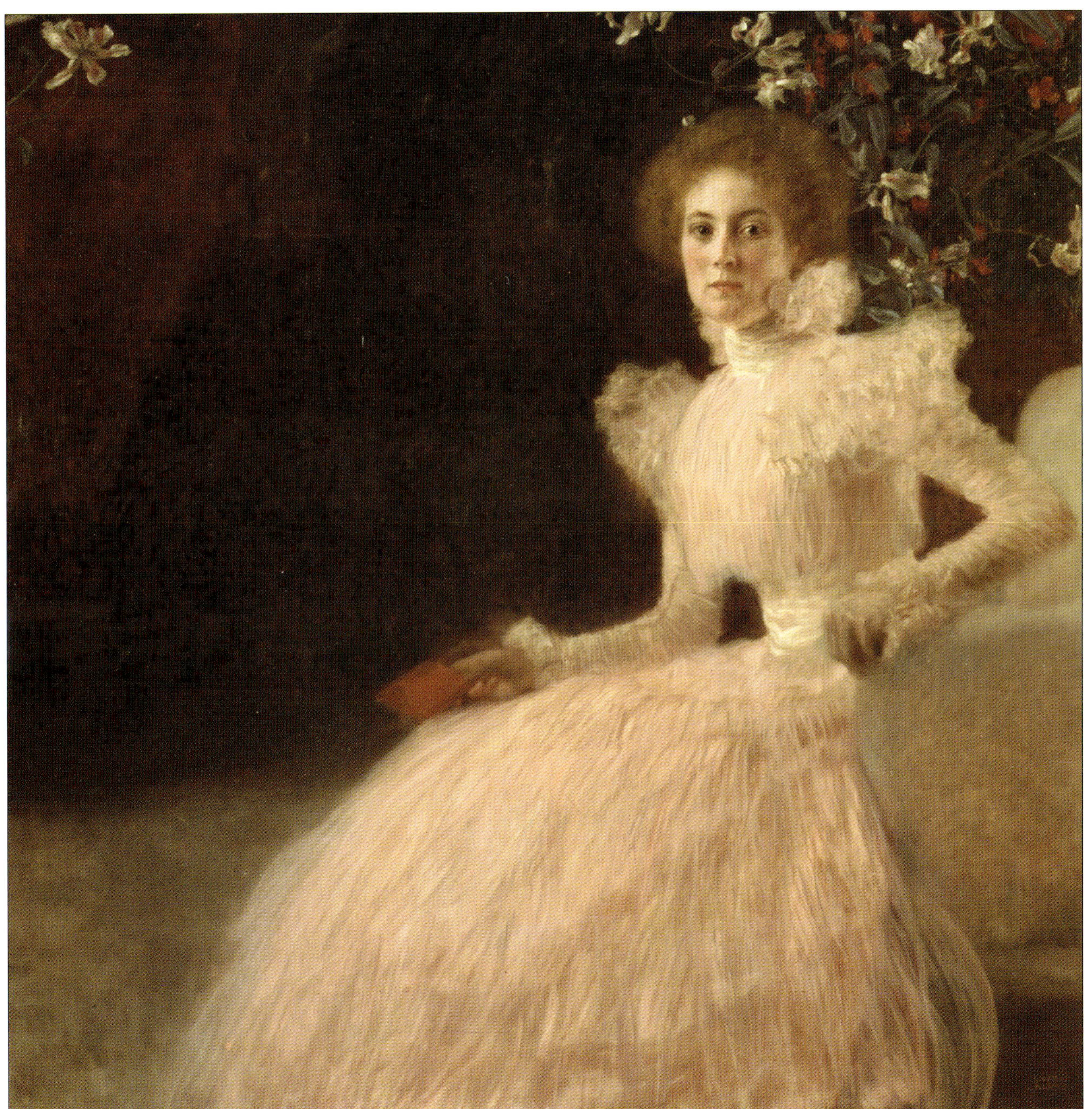

# COVER OF 'VER SACRUM'

*The journal of the Viennese Secession, depicting Theseus and the Minotaur, at the time of the first Secession exhibition in Vienna,
Lithograph. 1898. Wien Museum Karlsplatz, Vienna, Austria.*

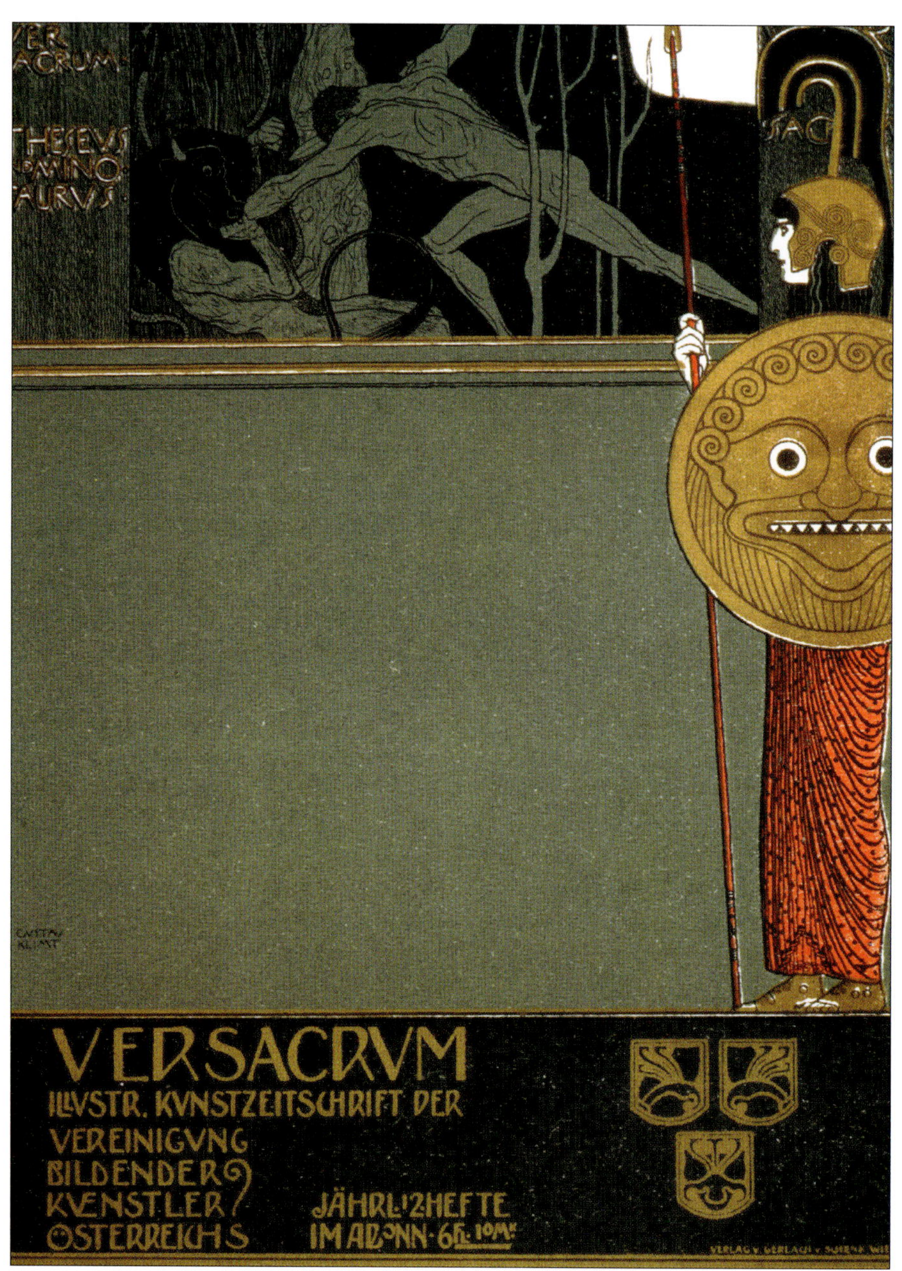

*Oil on canvas. 1899. Österreichische Nationalbibliothek, Vienna, Austria. 252 x 56 cm.*

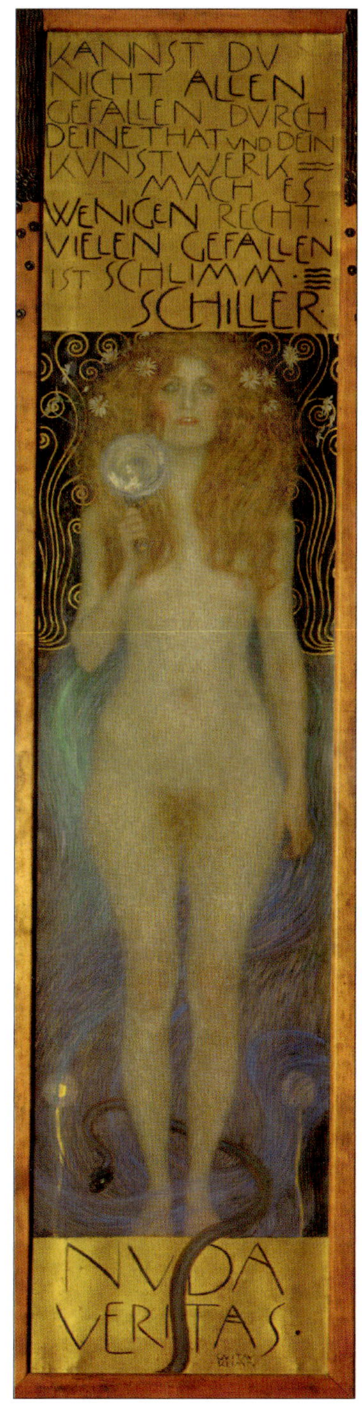

# HELENE KLIMT (KLIMT'S NIECE)

*Oil on card. 1898. Private collection.*
*60 x 40 cm.*

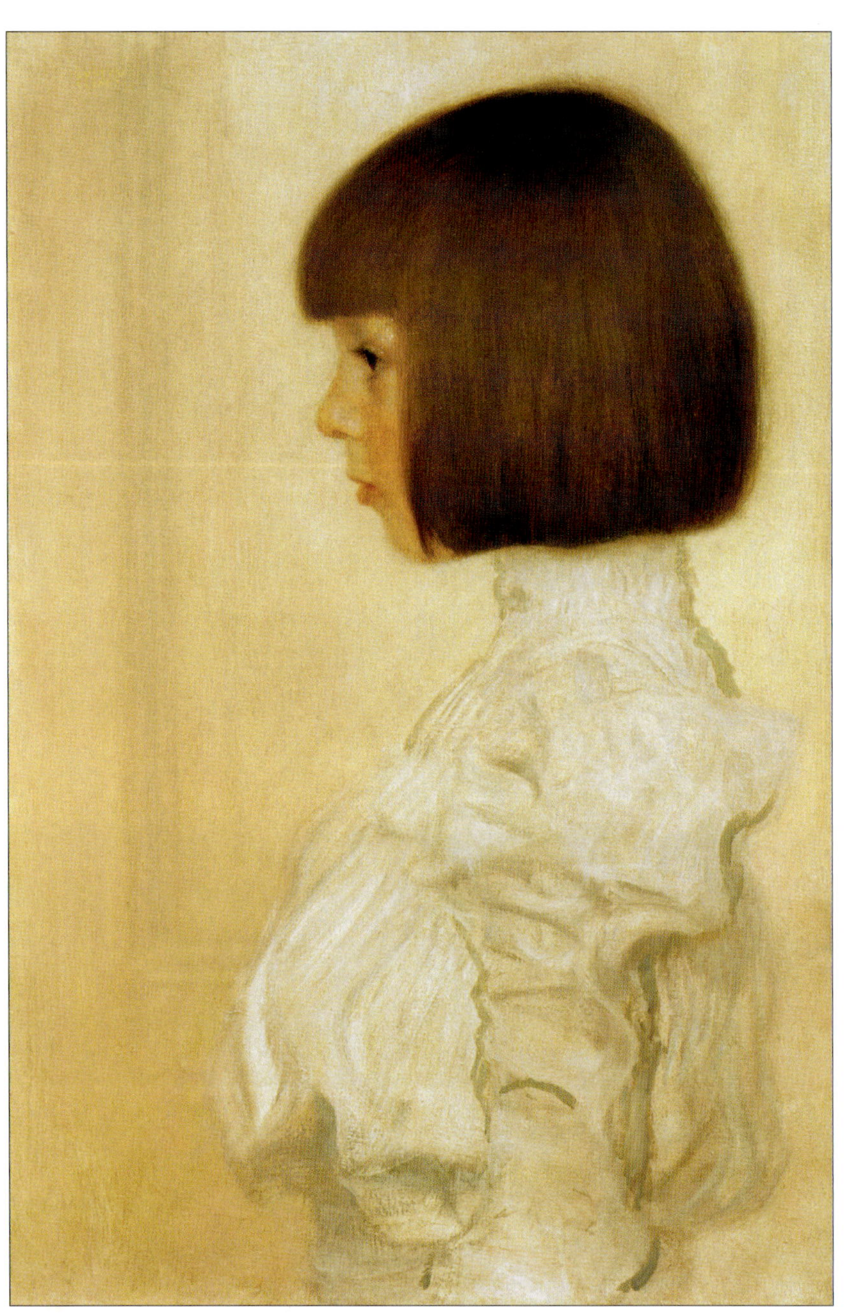

# PORTRAIT OF SERENE LEDERER

*Oil on canvas. 1899. Metropolitan Museum of Art, New York.*
*188 x 83 cm.*

# AFTER THE RAIN

*Oil on canvas. 1899. Österreichische Galerie Belvedere, Vienna, Austria.*
*80 x 40 cm.*

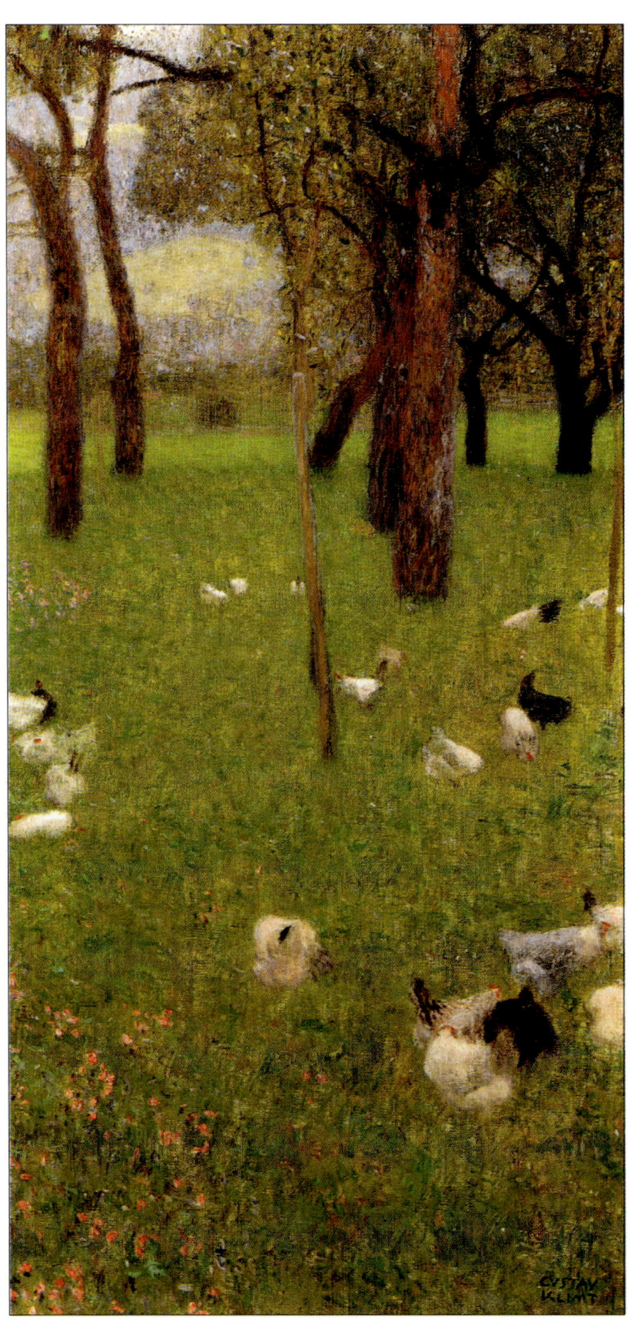

*Oil on canvas. 1899. Zentralsparkasse-Bank, Vienna, Austria.*
*82 x 52 cm.*

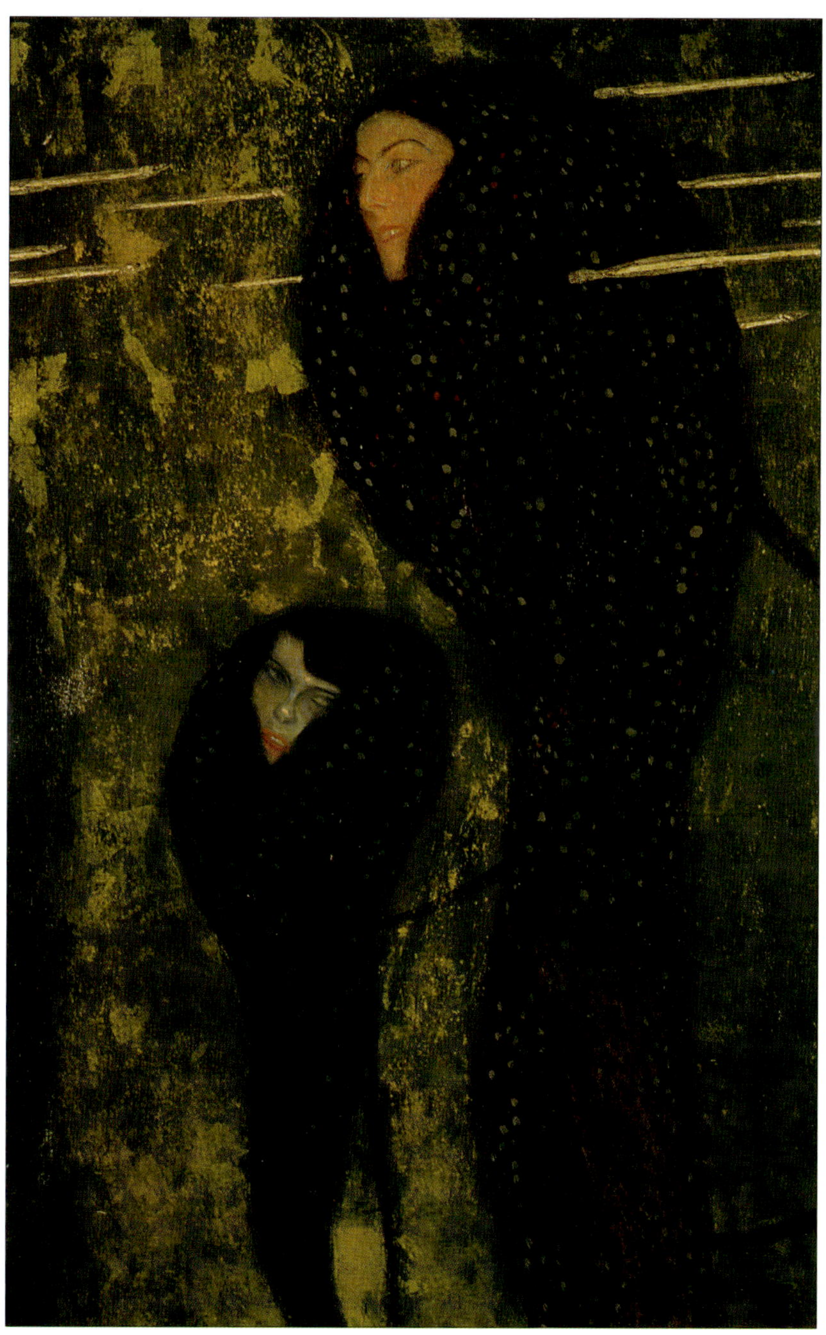

# THE SWAMP

*Oil on canvas. 1900. Private collection.*
*80 x 80 cm.*

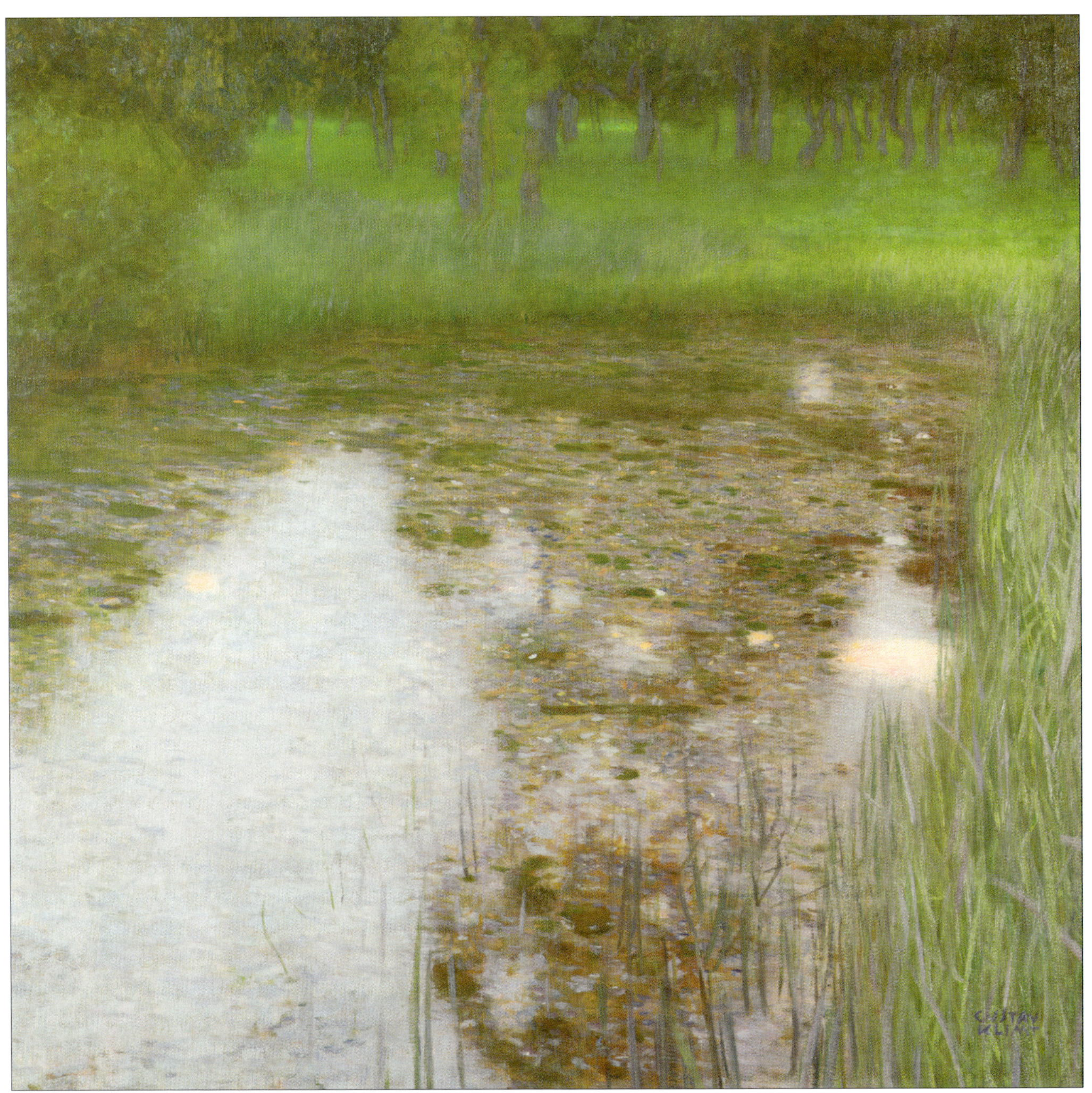

*Oil on canvas. 1900. Private collection.*
*80 x 81 cm.*

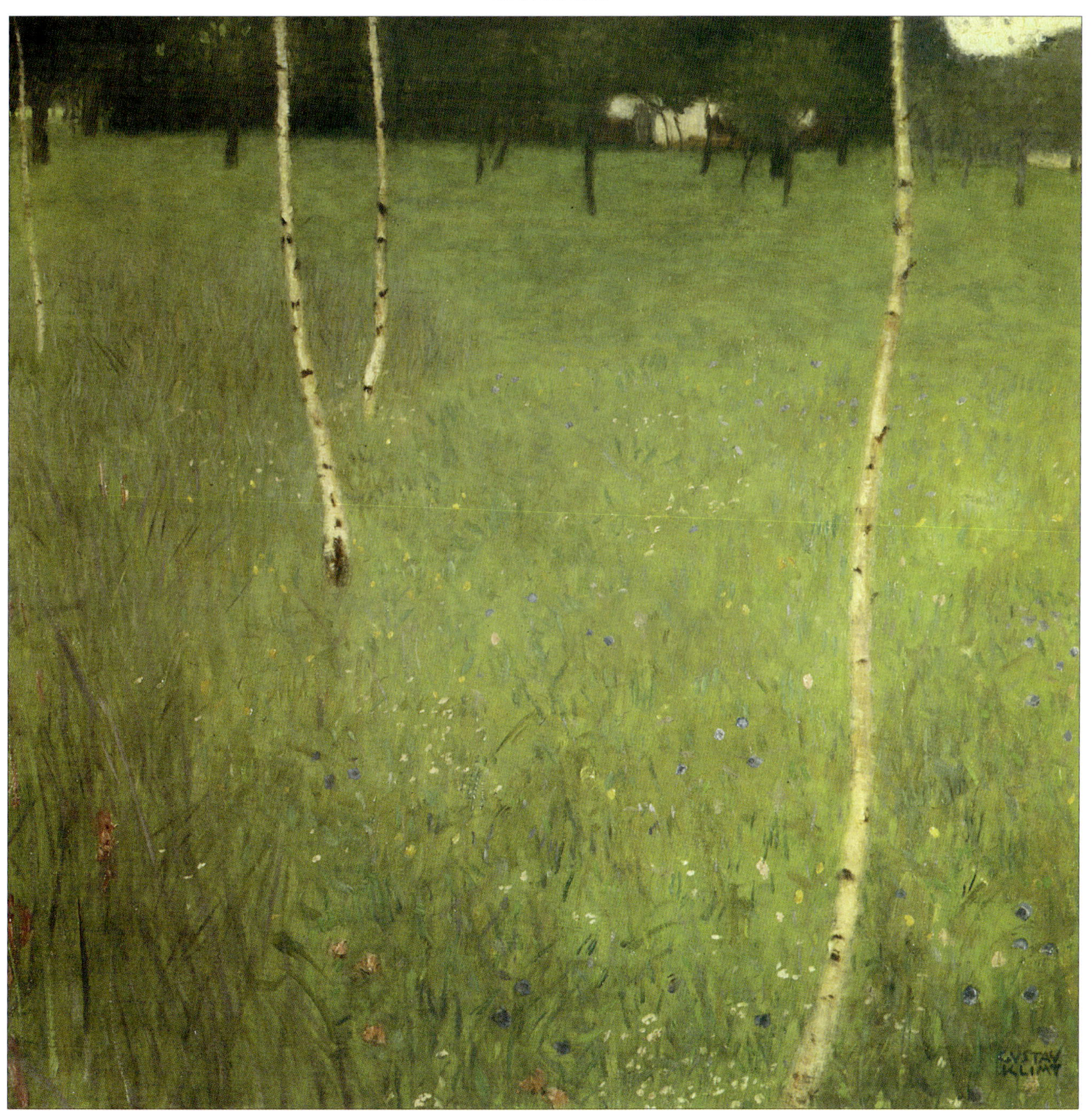

# BEECH FOREST

*Oil on canvas. 1900.*

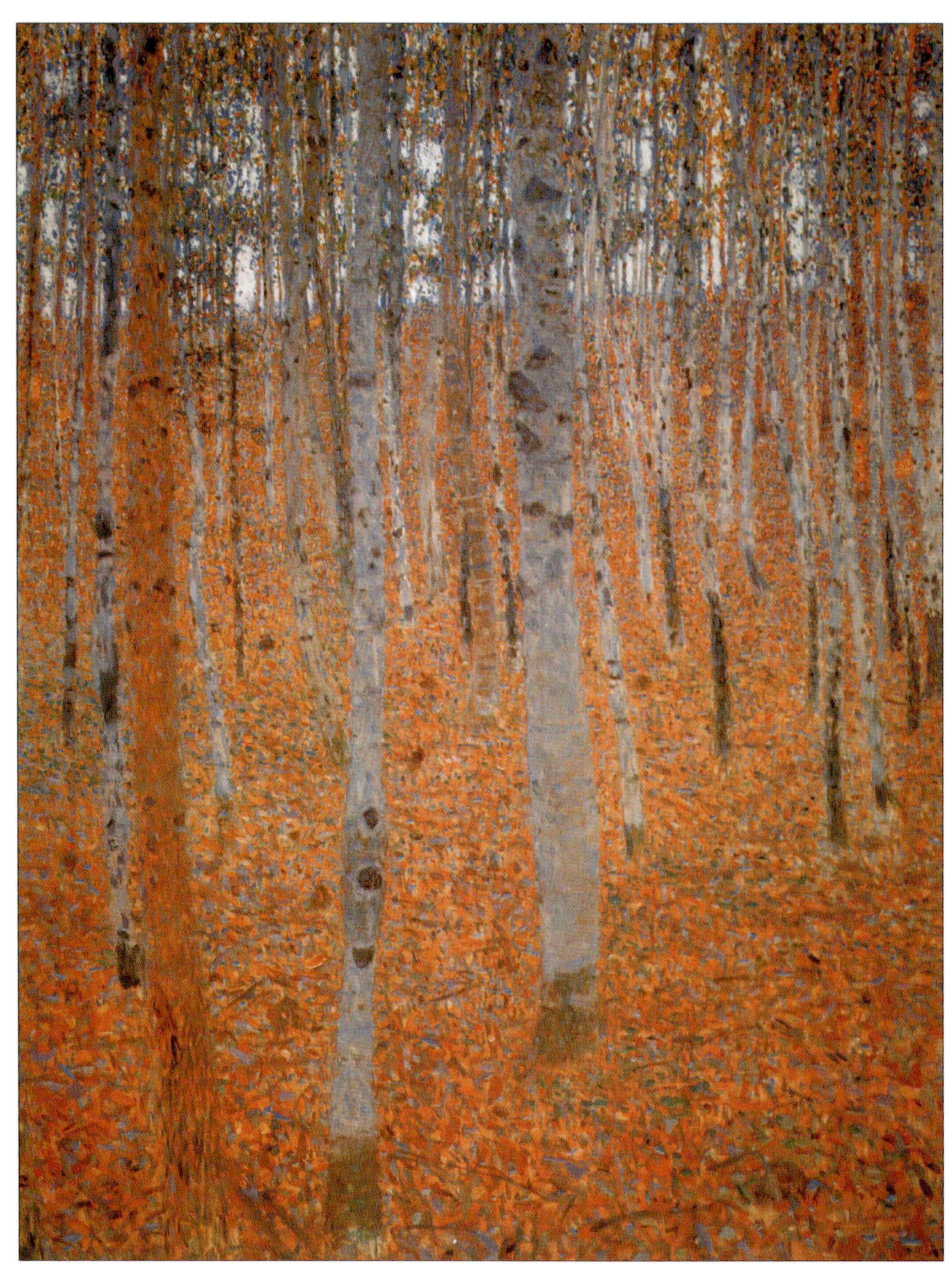

*Oil on canvas. 1901. Private collection.*
*90 x 90 cm.*

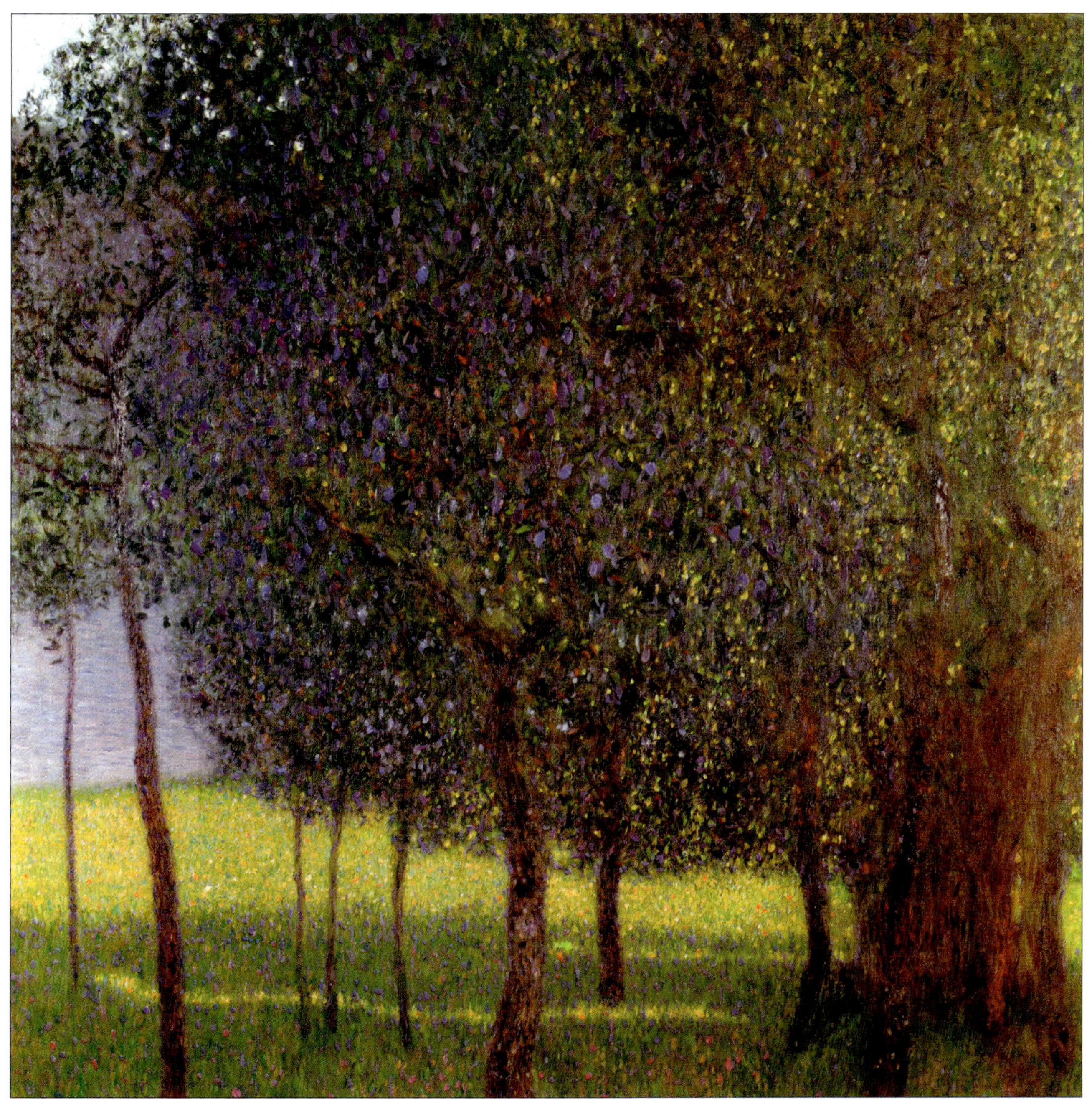

# THE BIRCH WOOD

*Oil on canvas. 1903. Private collection.*
*110 x 110 cm.*

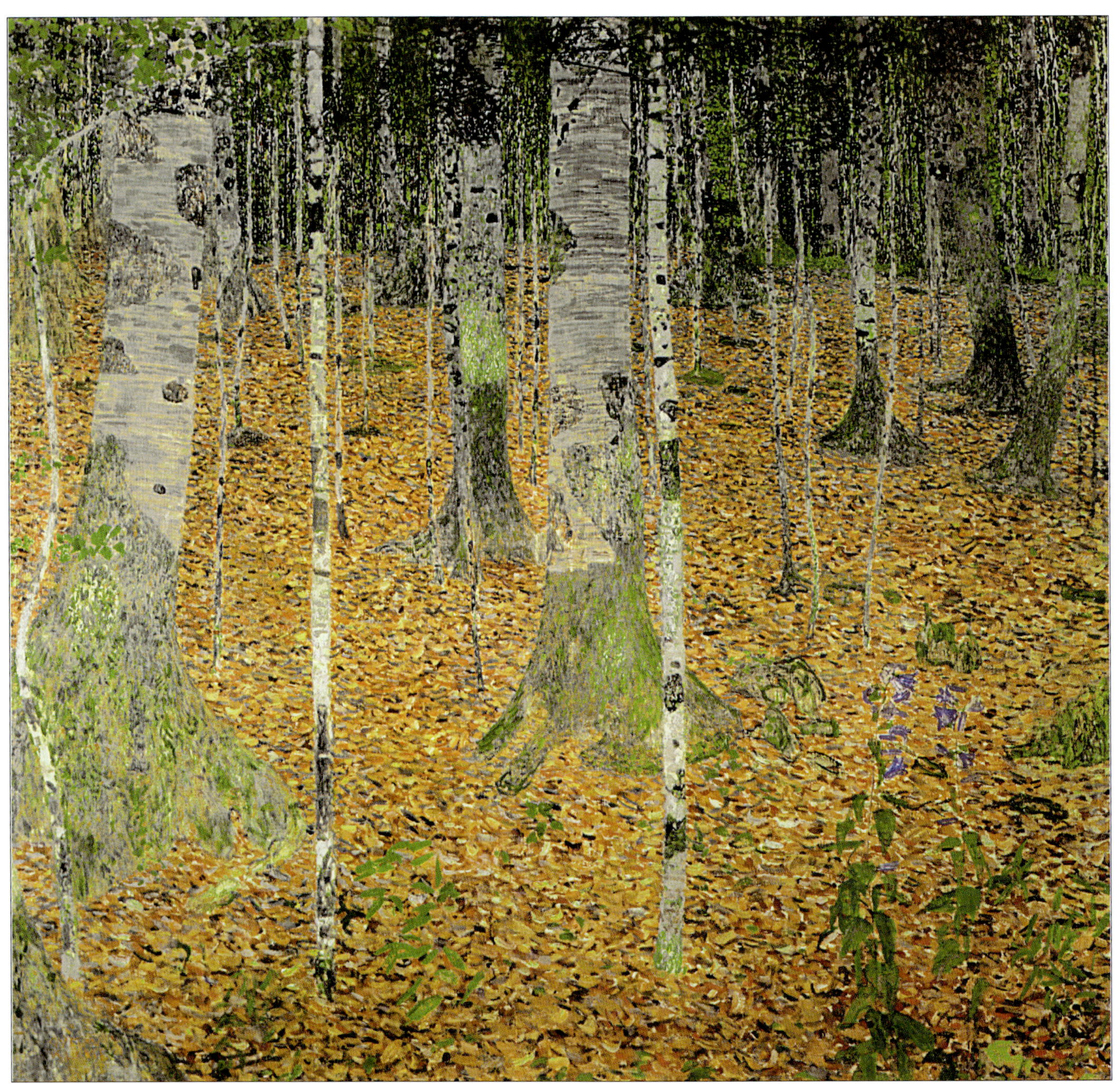

# PEAR TREE



*Oil and casein on canvas. 1903.*
*Busch-Reisinger Museum, Harvard University Art Museum, USA. 101 x 101 cm.*

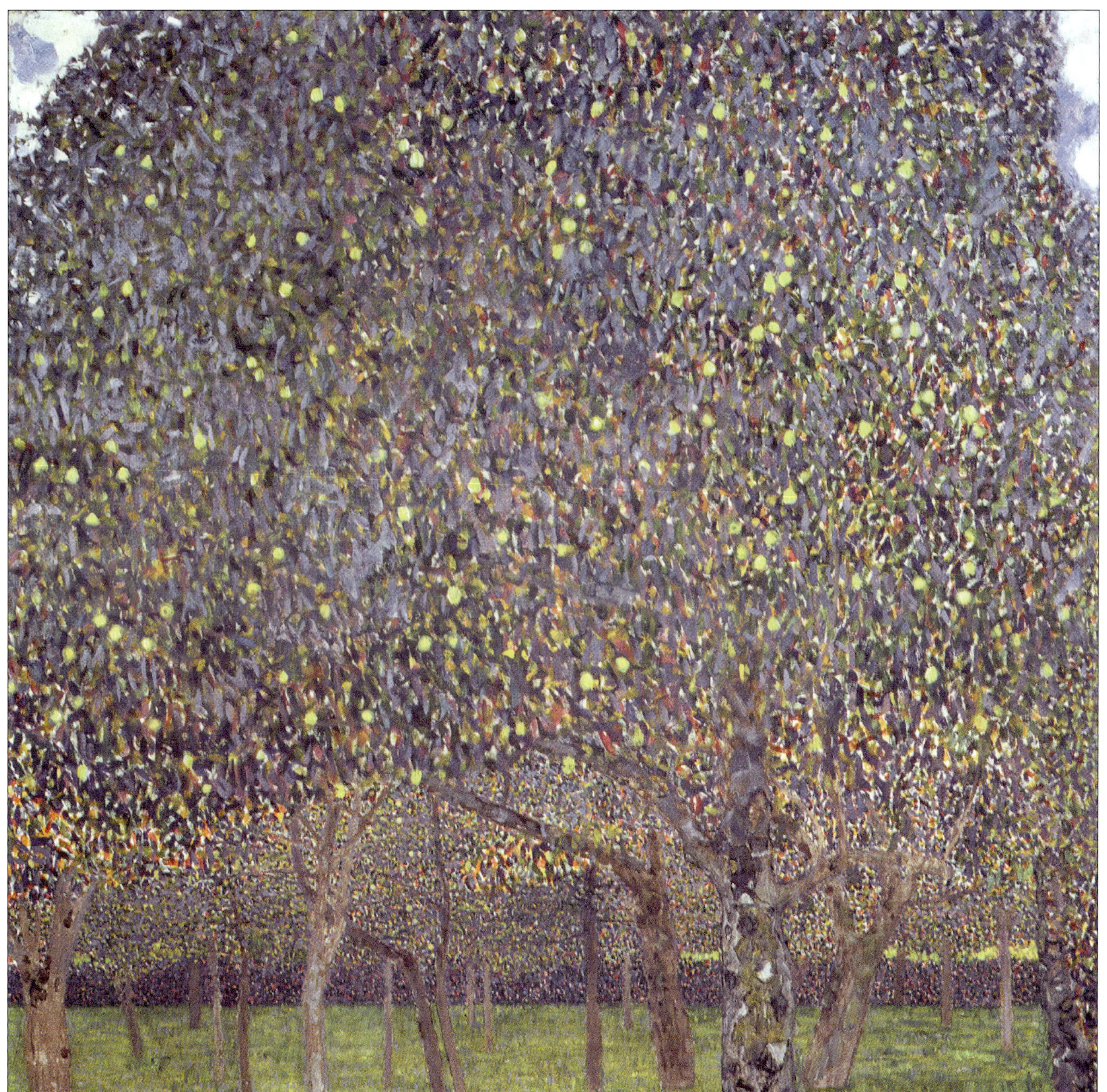

# ROSES UNDER THE TREES

*Oil on canvas. c.1905. Musée d'Orsay, Paris, France. 110 x 110 cm.*

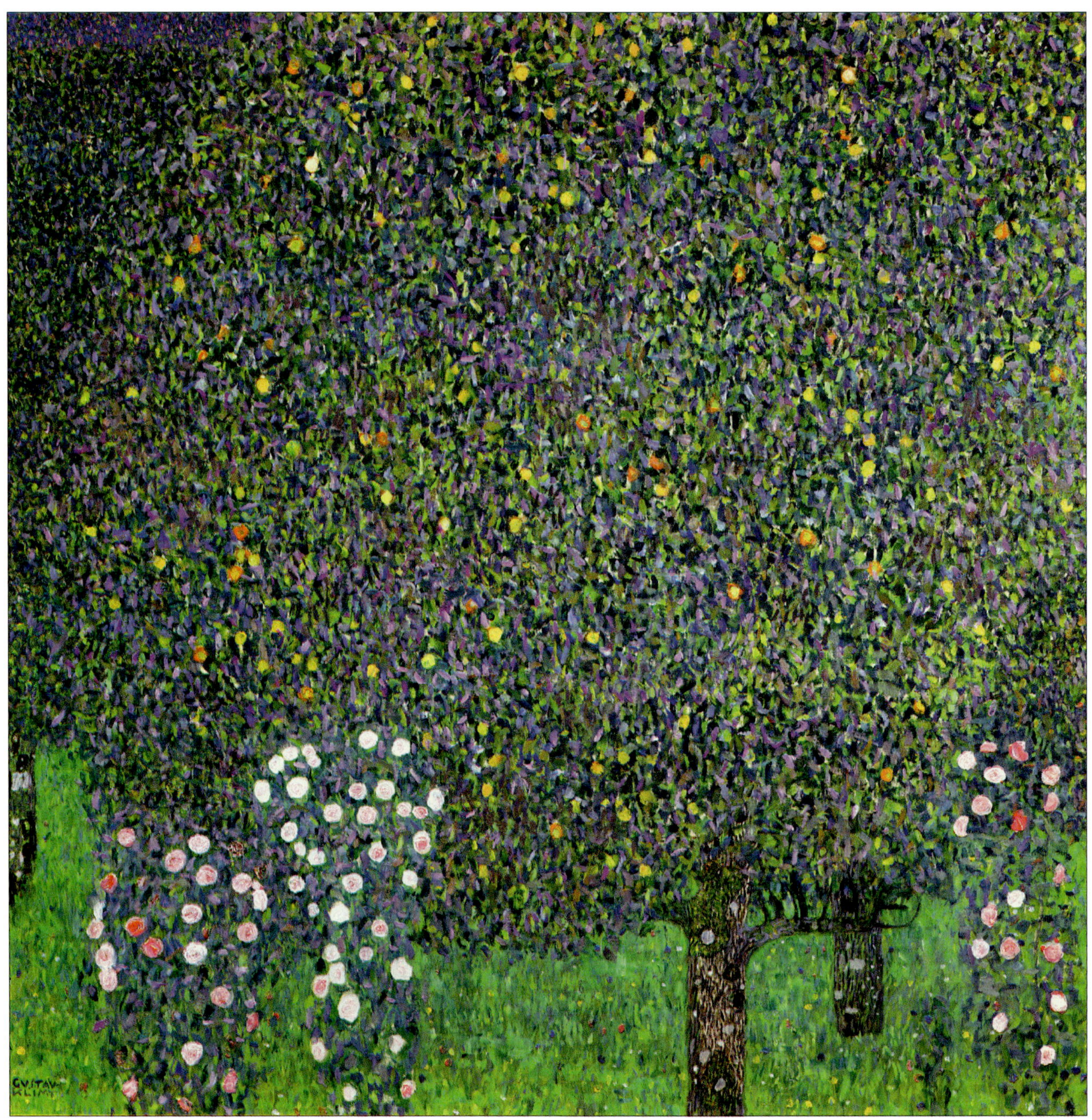

# FLOWER GARDEN

*Oil on canvas. 1905–06. Národní Galerie, Prague, Czech Republic.*

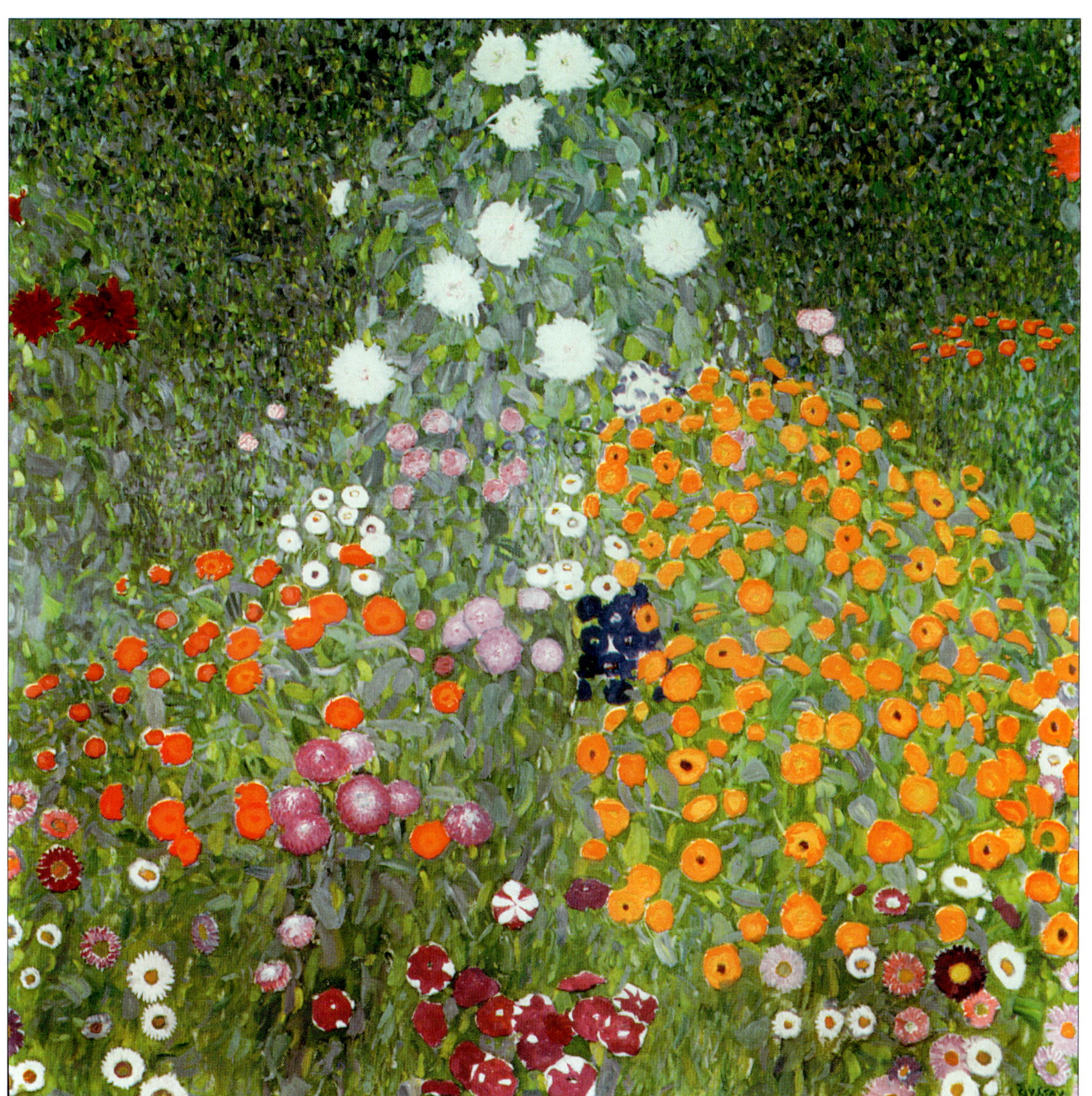

# HYGIEIA

*Detail from Medicine. 1900–7. Destroyed by fire at Immendorf Castle in 1945.*

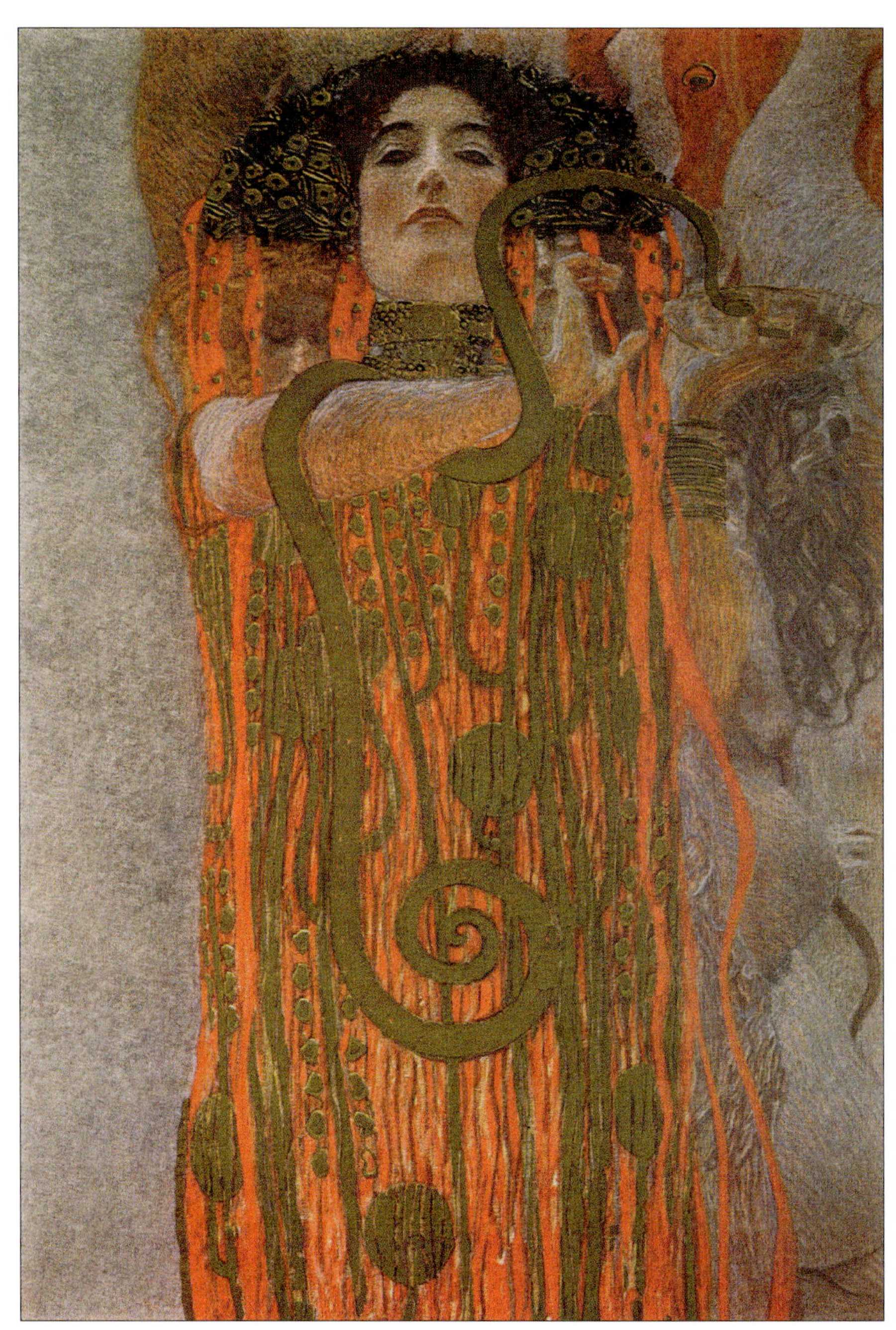

*Woodcut (illustration in Allegorien und Embleme). 1901. Private collection. 430 x 300 cm.*

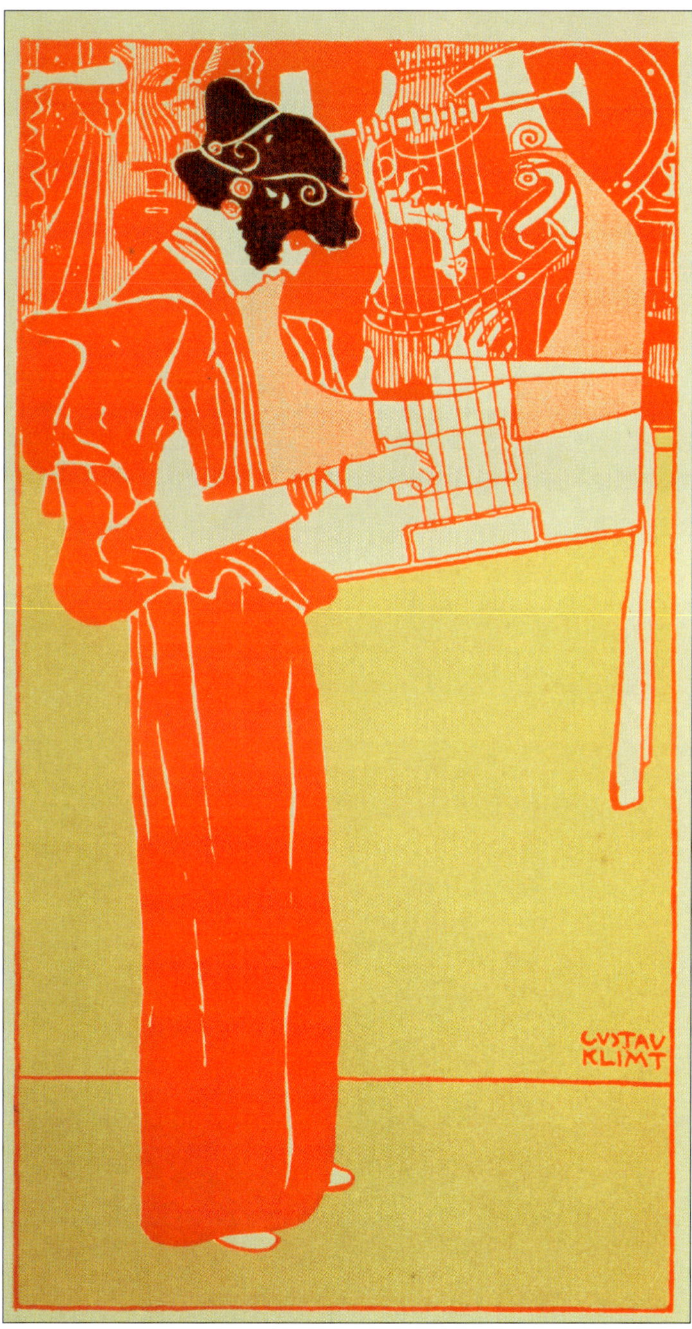

# JUDITH

*Oil on canvas. 1901. Osterreichische Galerie Belvedere, Vienna, Austria. 84 x 42 cm.*

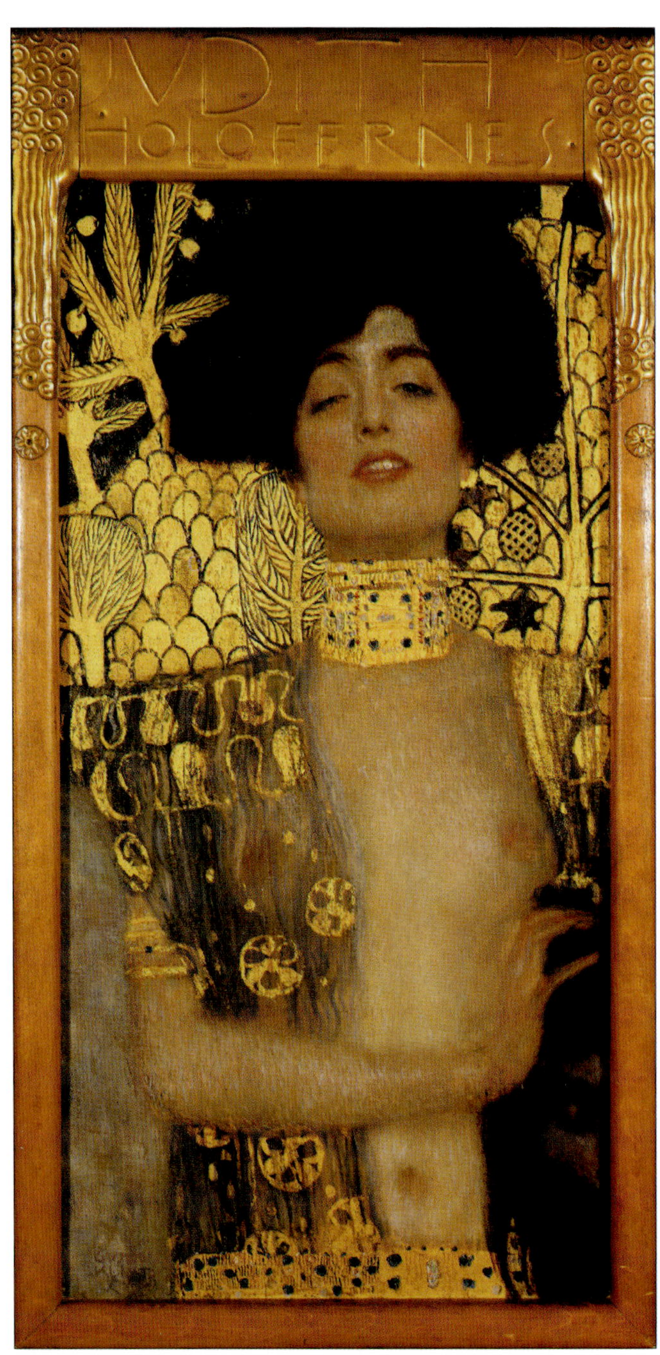

# GOLDFISH

*Oil on canvas. 1901–02. Private collection. 181 x 66.5 cm.*

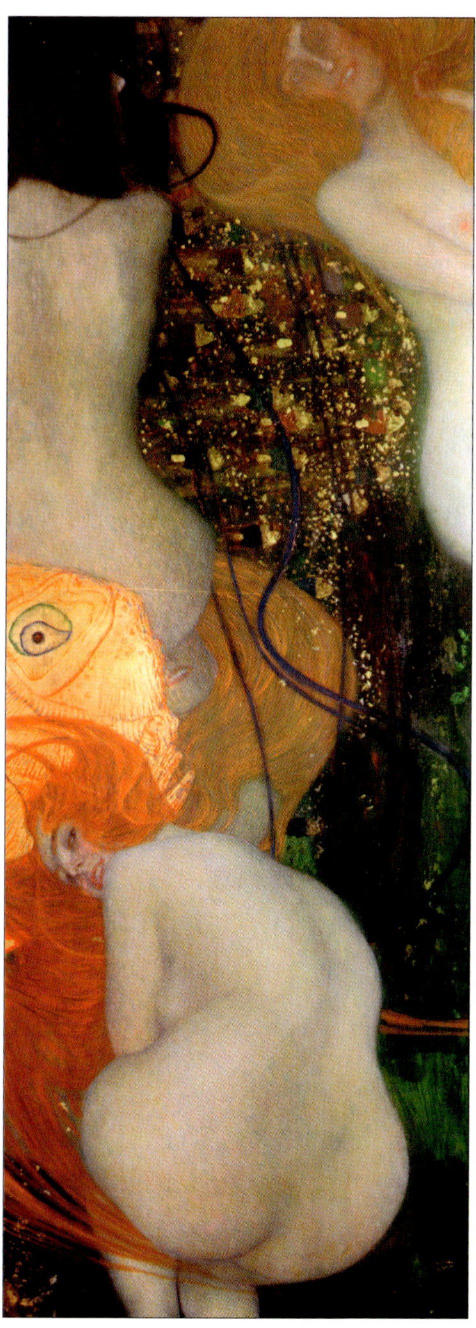

# THE BIG POPLAR II

*Oil on canvas. 1902–03. Private collection. 101 x 101 cm.*

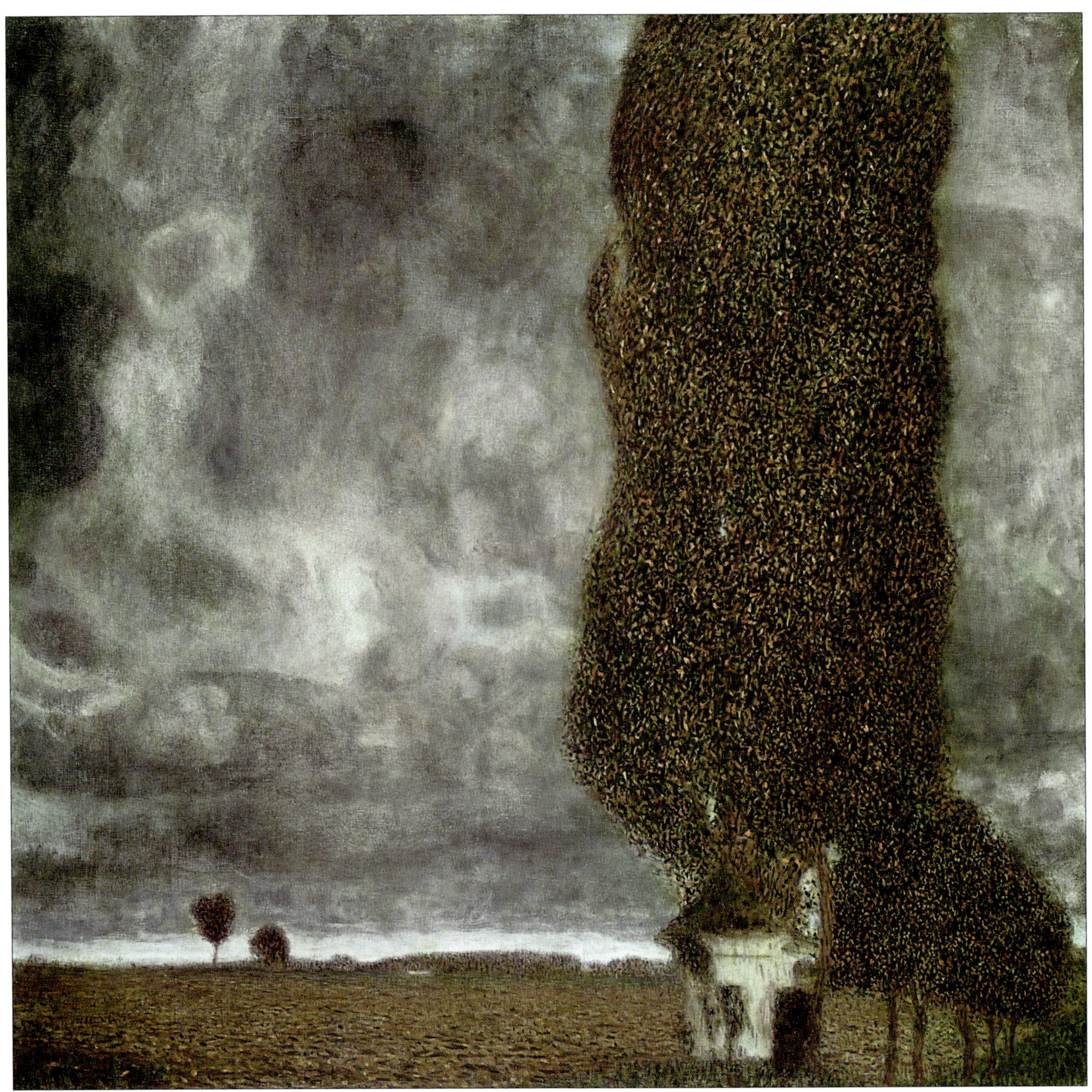

# EMILIE FLOEGE

*Oil on canvas. 1902. Wien Museum Karlsplatz, Vienna, Austria. 181 x 84 cm.*

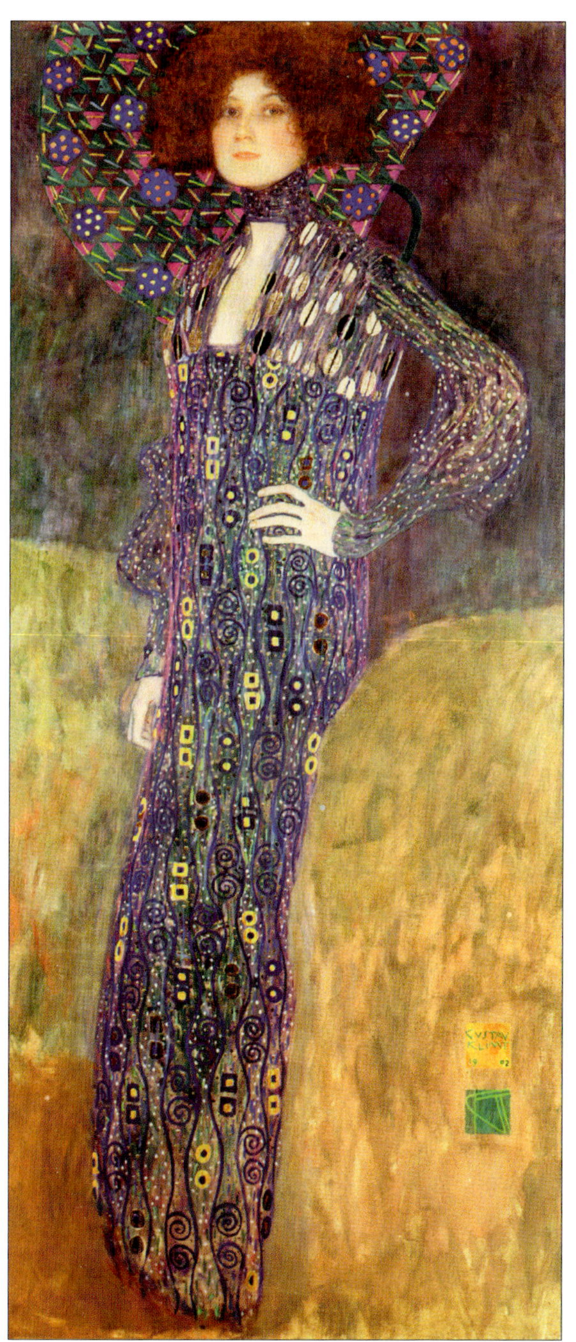

# HOPE I

*Oil on canvas. 1903. National Gallery of Canada, Ottawa. 189 x 67 cm.*

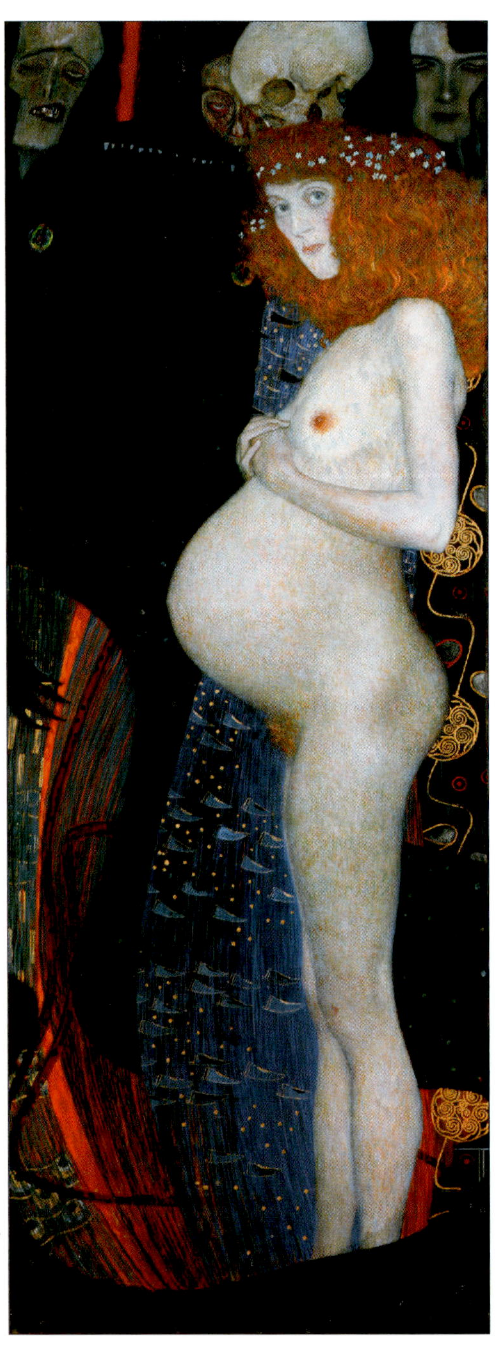

*Oil on canvas. 1903. Private collection. 100 x 100 cm.*

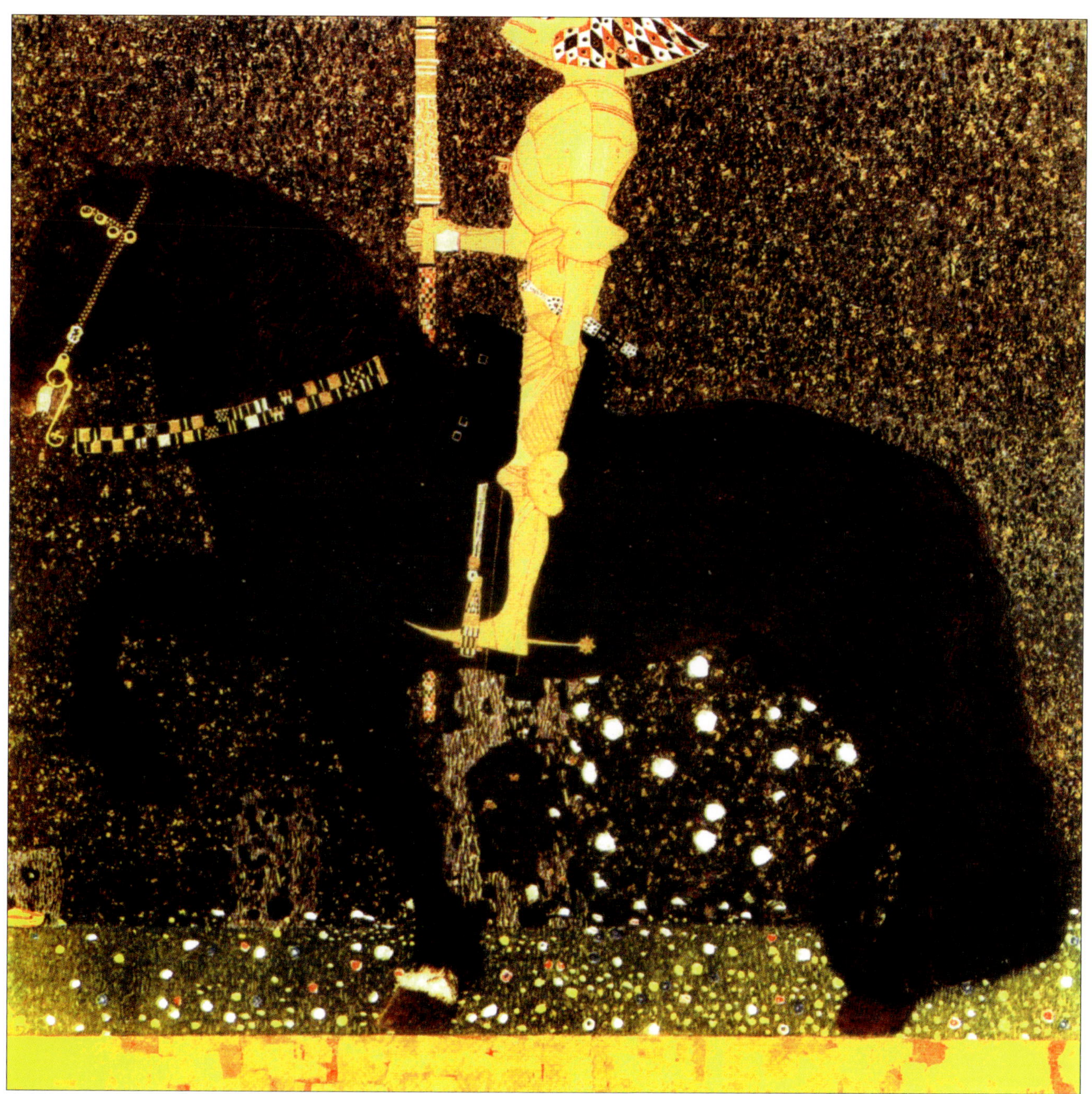

# PORTRAIT OF HERMINE GALLIA

*Oil on canvas. 1904. National Gallery, London, UK. 170.5 x 96.5 cm.*

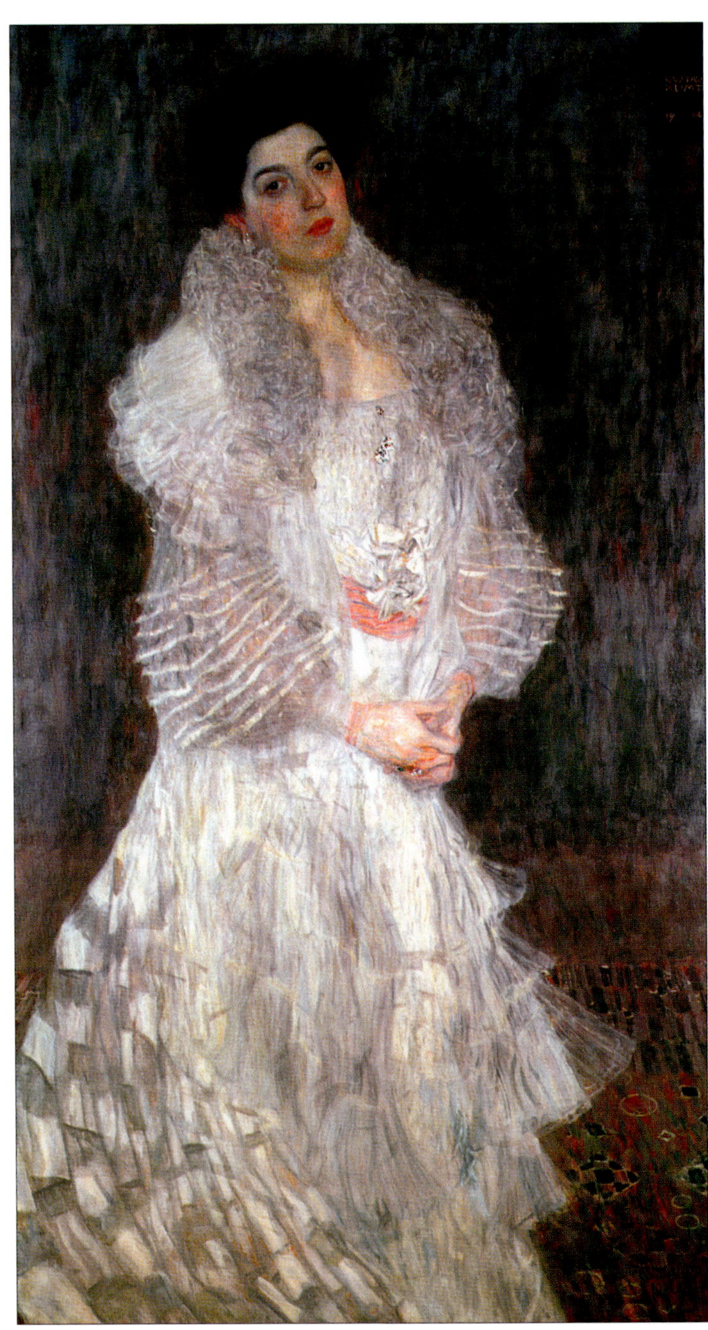

*Oil on canvas. 1904–07.*
*Österreichische Galerie Belvedere, Vienna, Austria.*

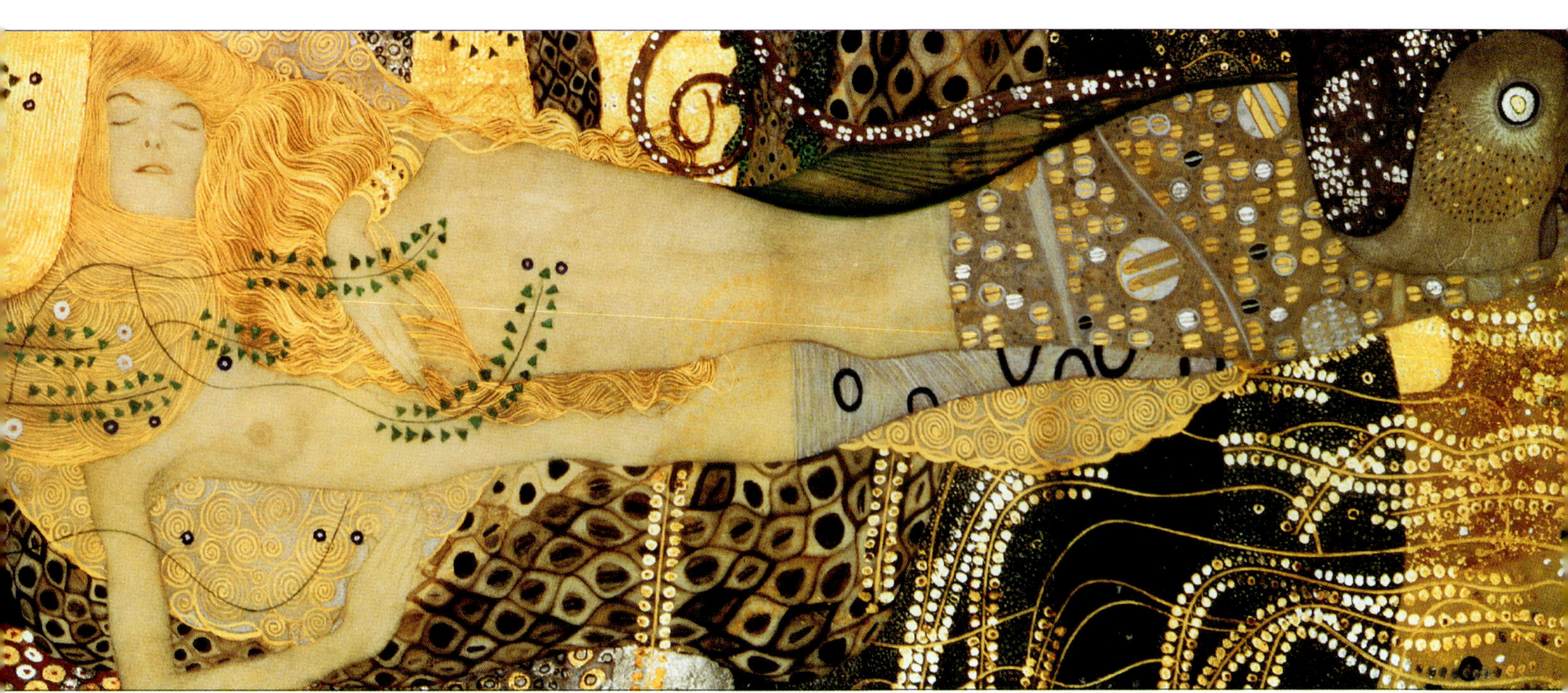

 **'ODE TO JOY' AND 'THE KISS TO THE WHOLE WORLD' FROM THE BEETHOVEN FRIEZE**

*Casein colour, gold leaf, semiprecious stone, plaster, charcoal and pencil on stucco ground. 1902.  Österreichische Galerie Belvedere, Vienna, Austria. 216 x 300 cm.*

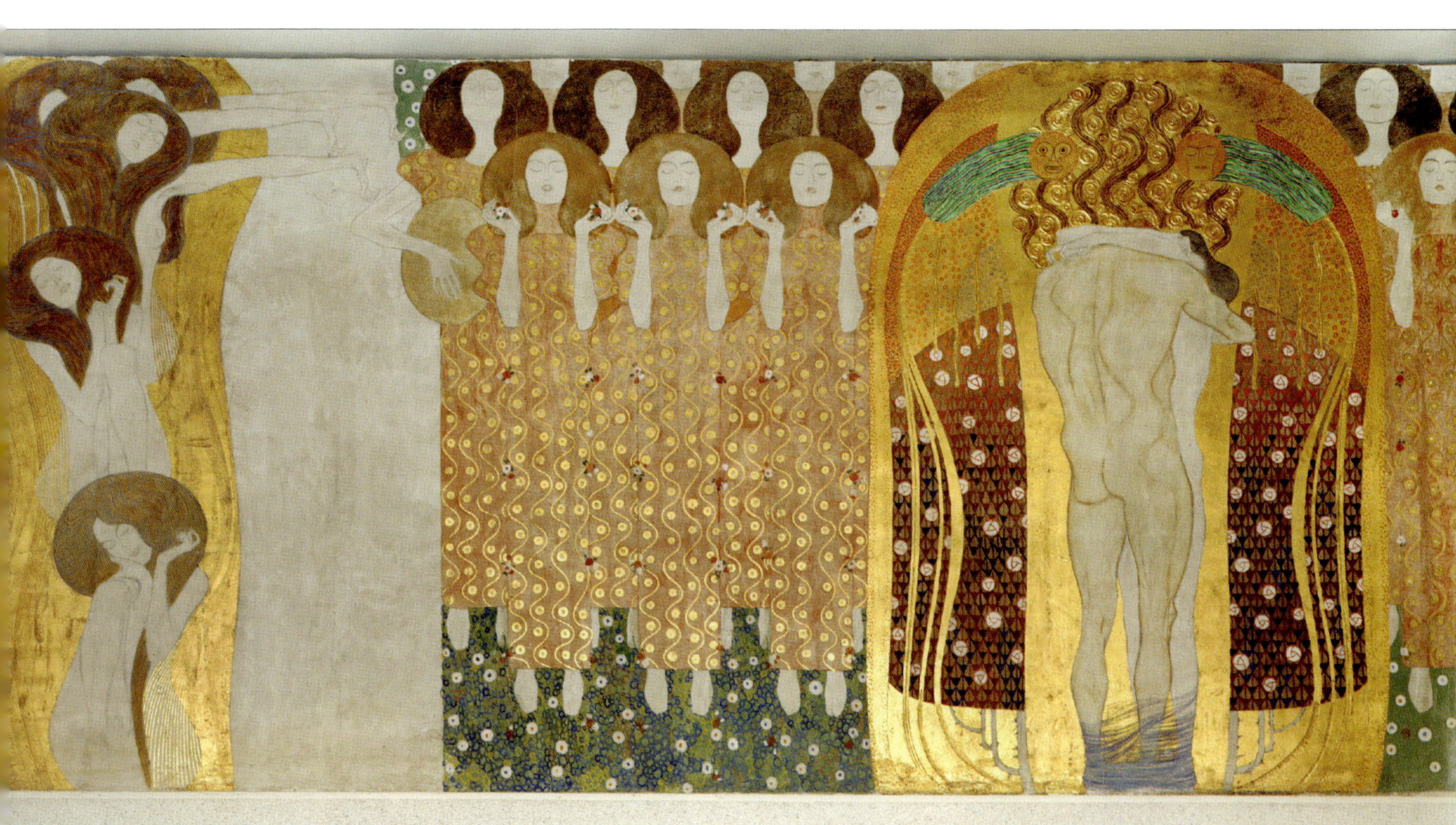

*Said to be the portrait of Gustav Mahler. 1902 fresco.*
*Österreichische Galerie Belvedere, Vienna, Austria.*

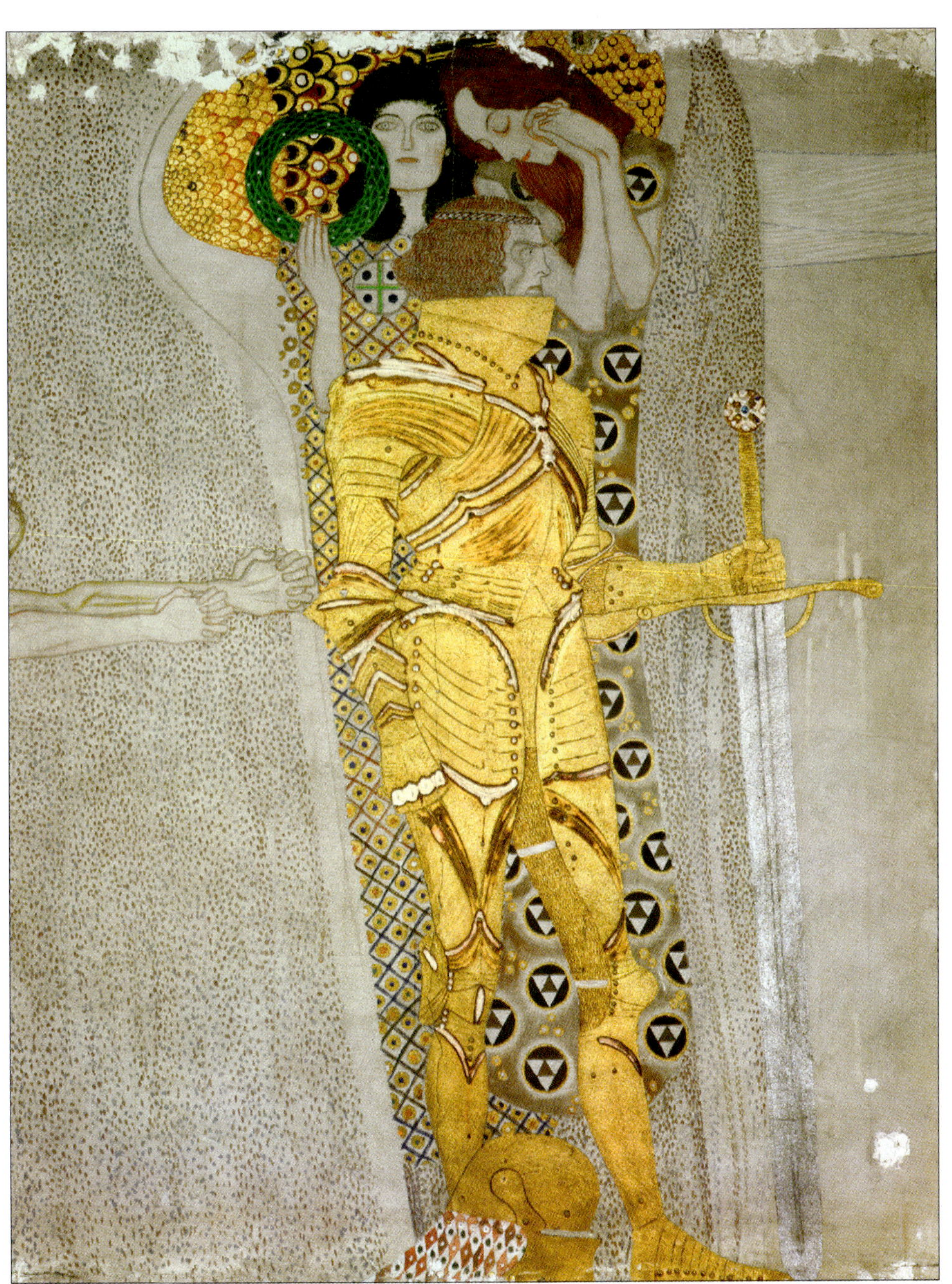

# 'GNAWING PERSONIFICATION' FROM THE BEETHOVEN FRIEZE

*Cassein on stucco. 1902.*
*Österreichische Galerie Belvedere, Vienna, Austria.*

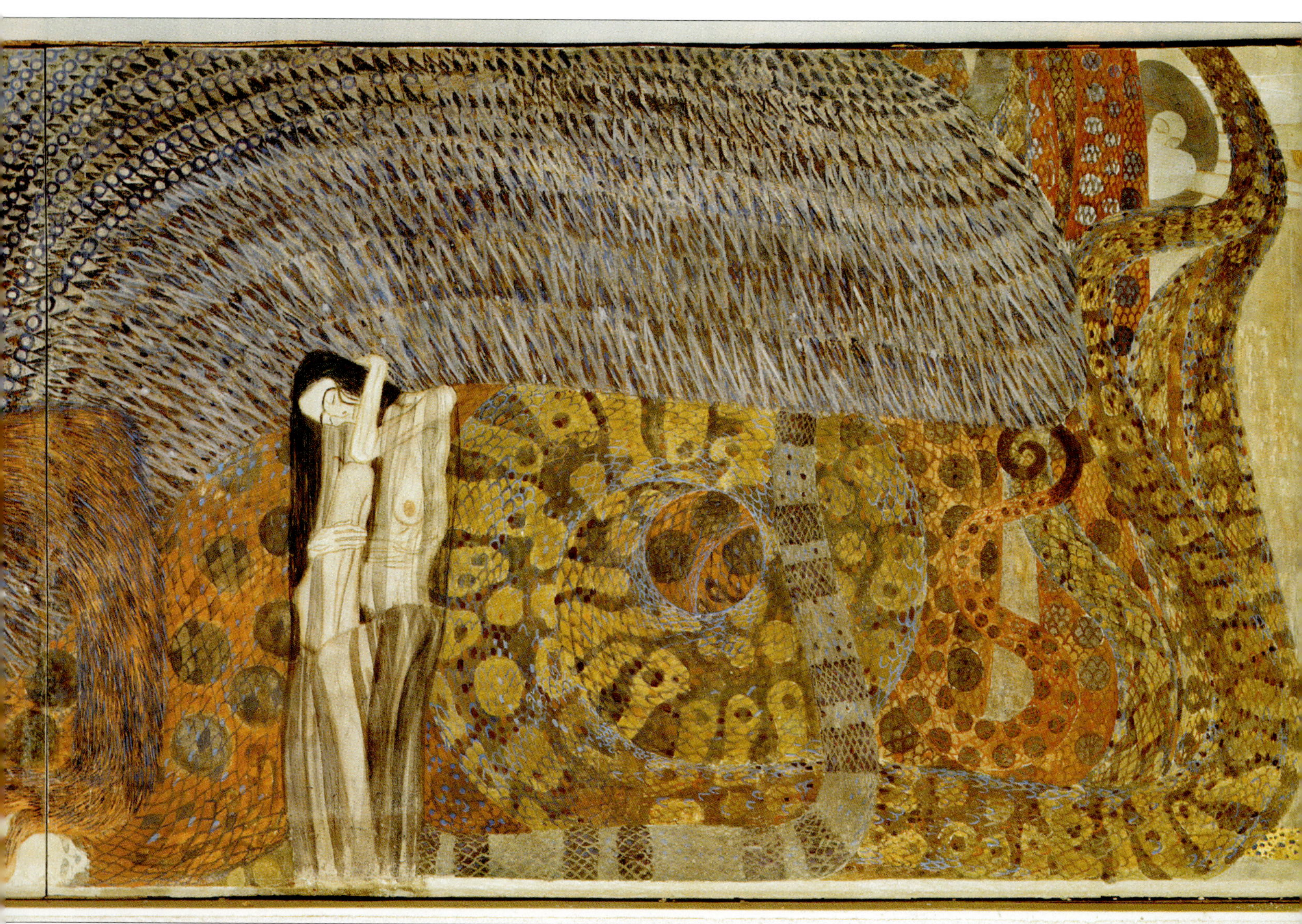

# STUDY FOR EXPECTATION

*Watercolour and gold on paper. c.1905–09.*
*MAK (Austrian Museum of Applied Arts) Vienna, Austria. 193 x 115 cm.*

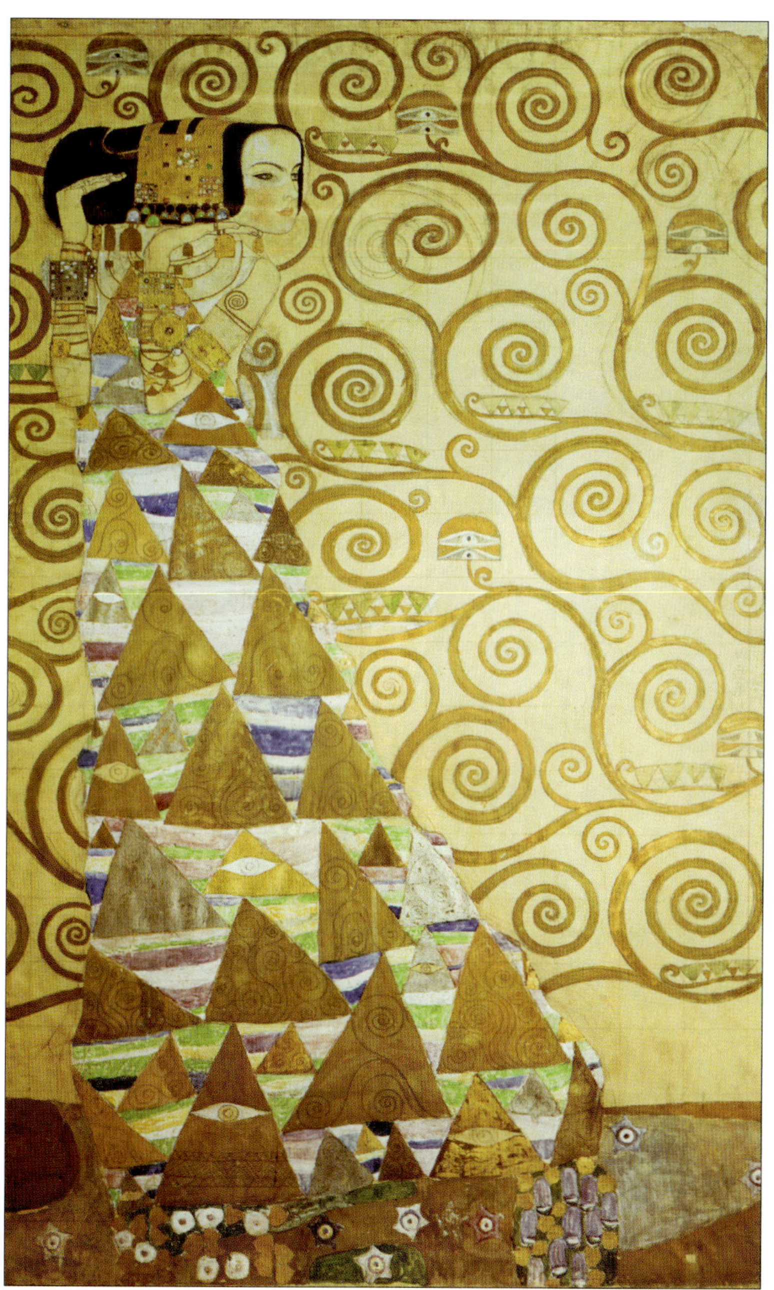

# TREE OF LIFE (STOCLET FRIEZE)

*Tempura/watercolour. c.1905–09.*
*MAK (Austrian Museum of Applied Arts) Vienna, Austria.*

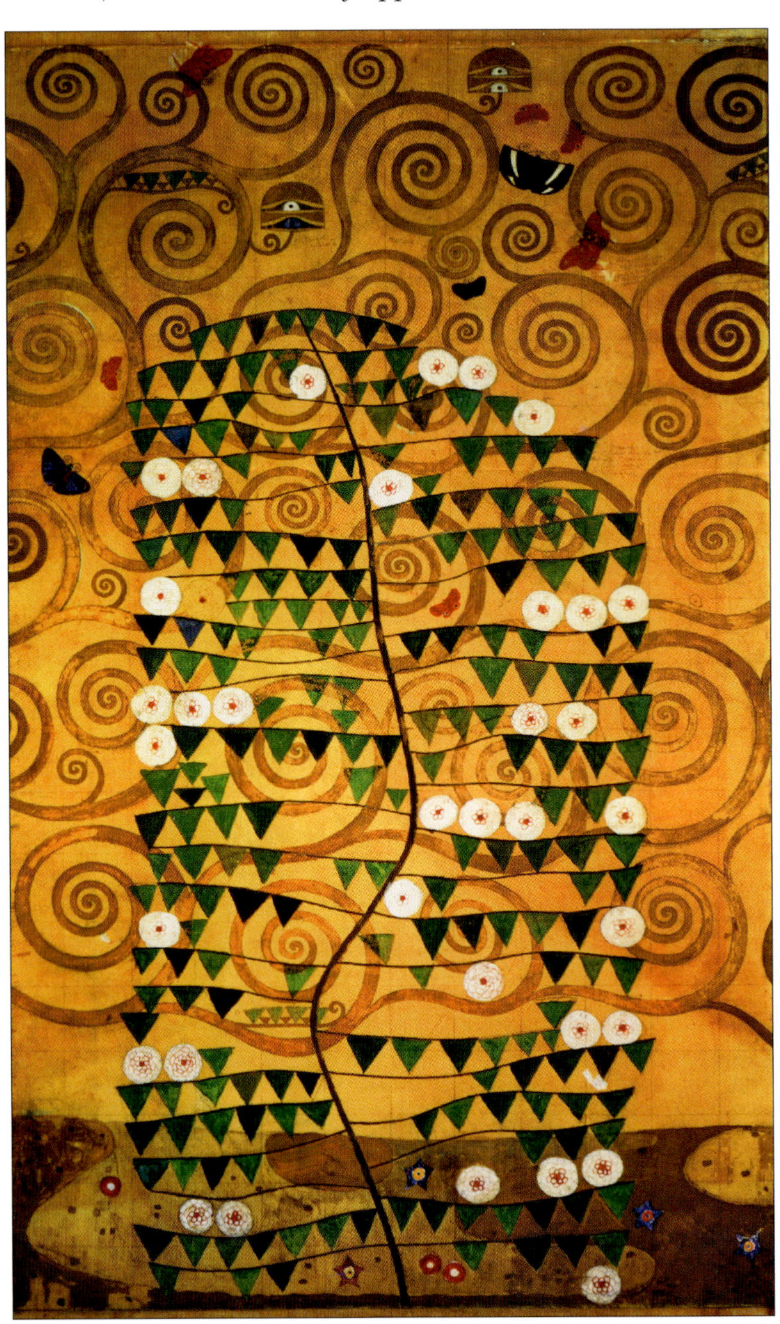

*Waterolour and gold on paper. c.1905–09 Musée des Beaux-Arts, Strasbourg. 194 x 121 cm.*

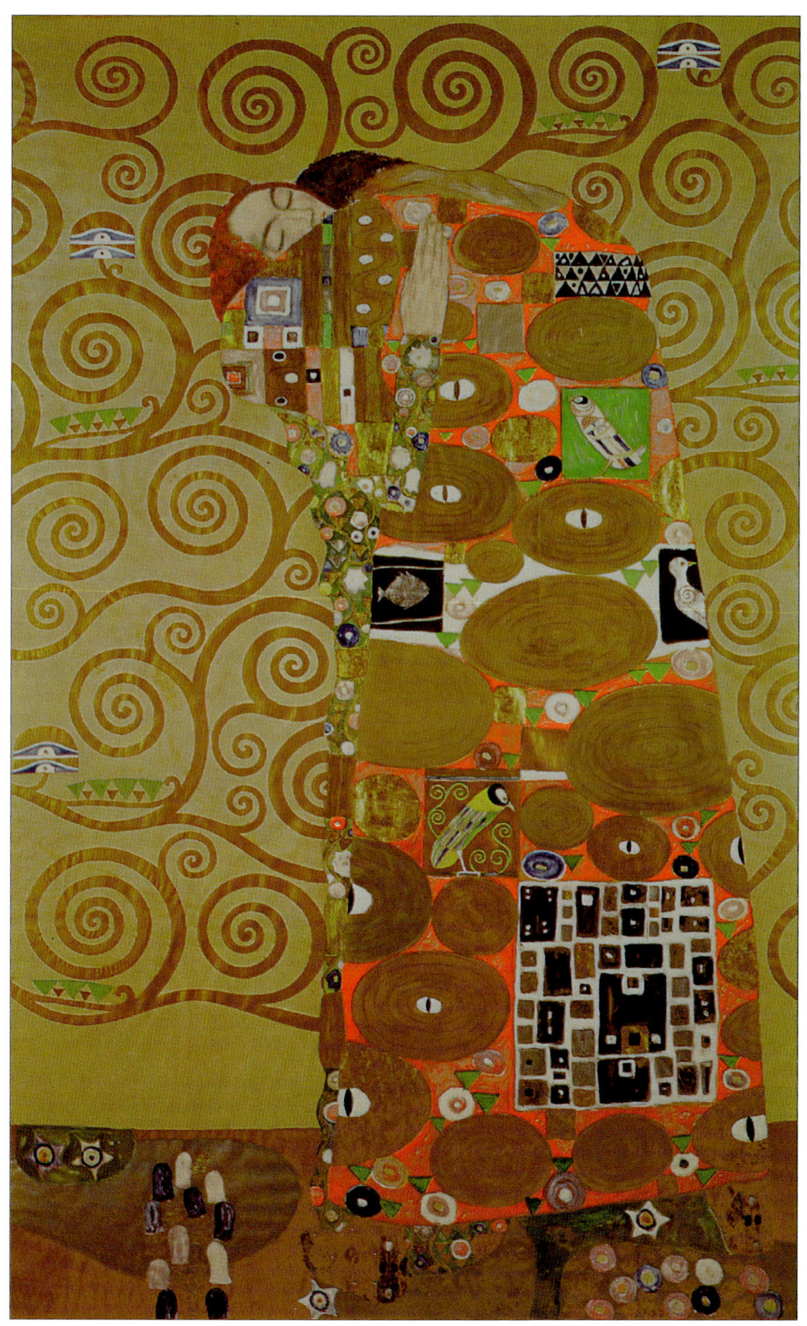

# FULFILMENT (STOCLET FRIEZE) *(Detail)*

*Tempura/watercolour. c.1905–09.*
*MAK (Austrian Museum of Applied Arts) Vienna, Austria.*
*118 x 192 cm.*

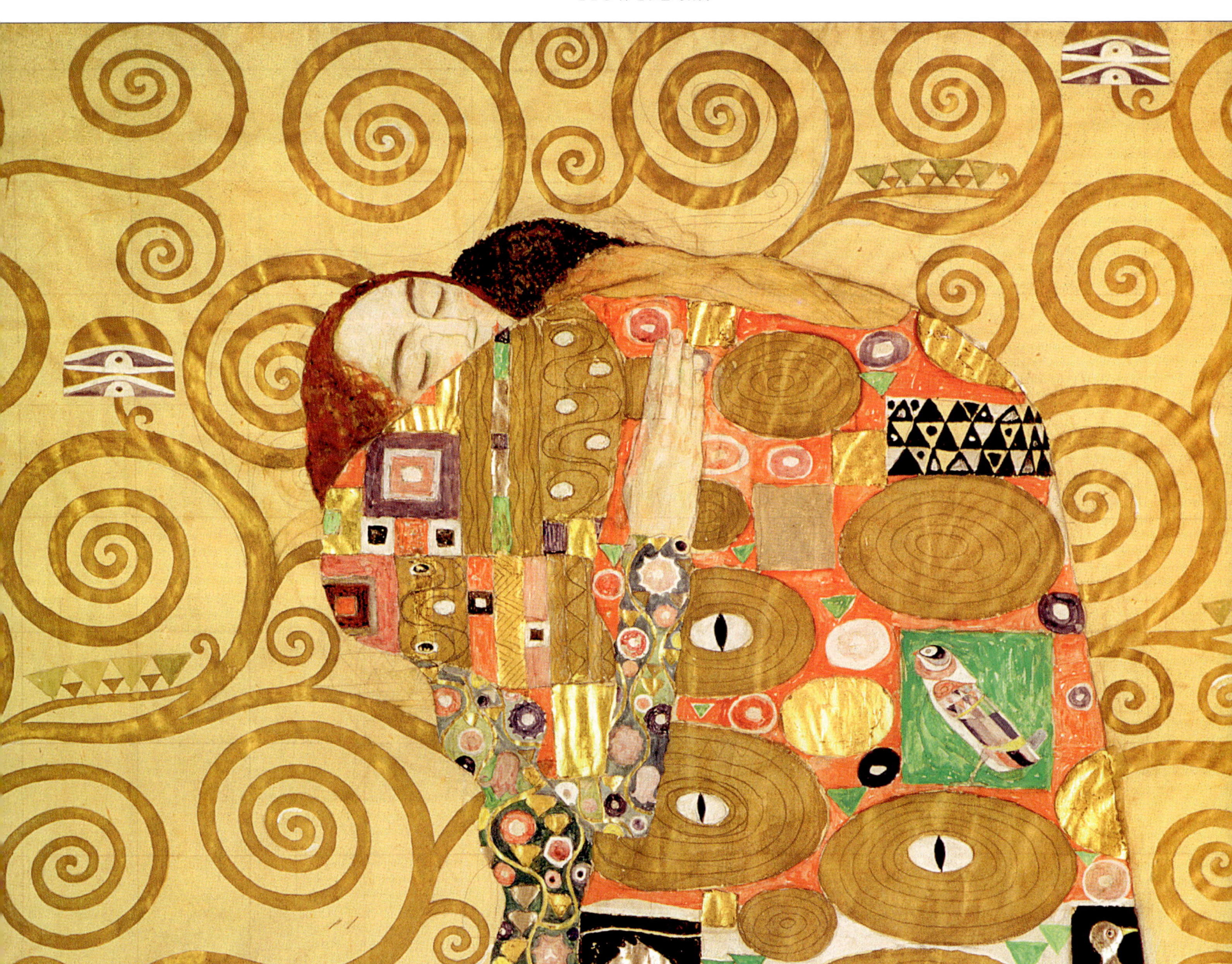

*Oil on canvas. 1905. Galleria Nazionale d'Arte Moderna, Rome, Italy. 178 x 198 cm.*

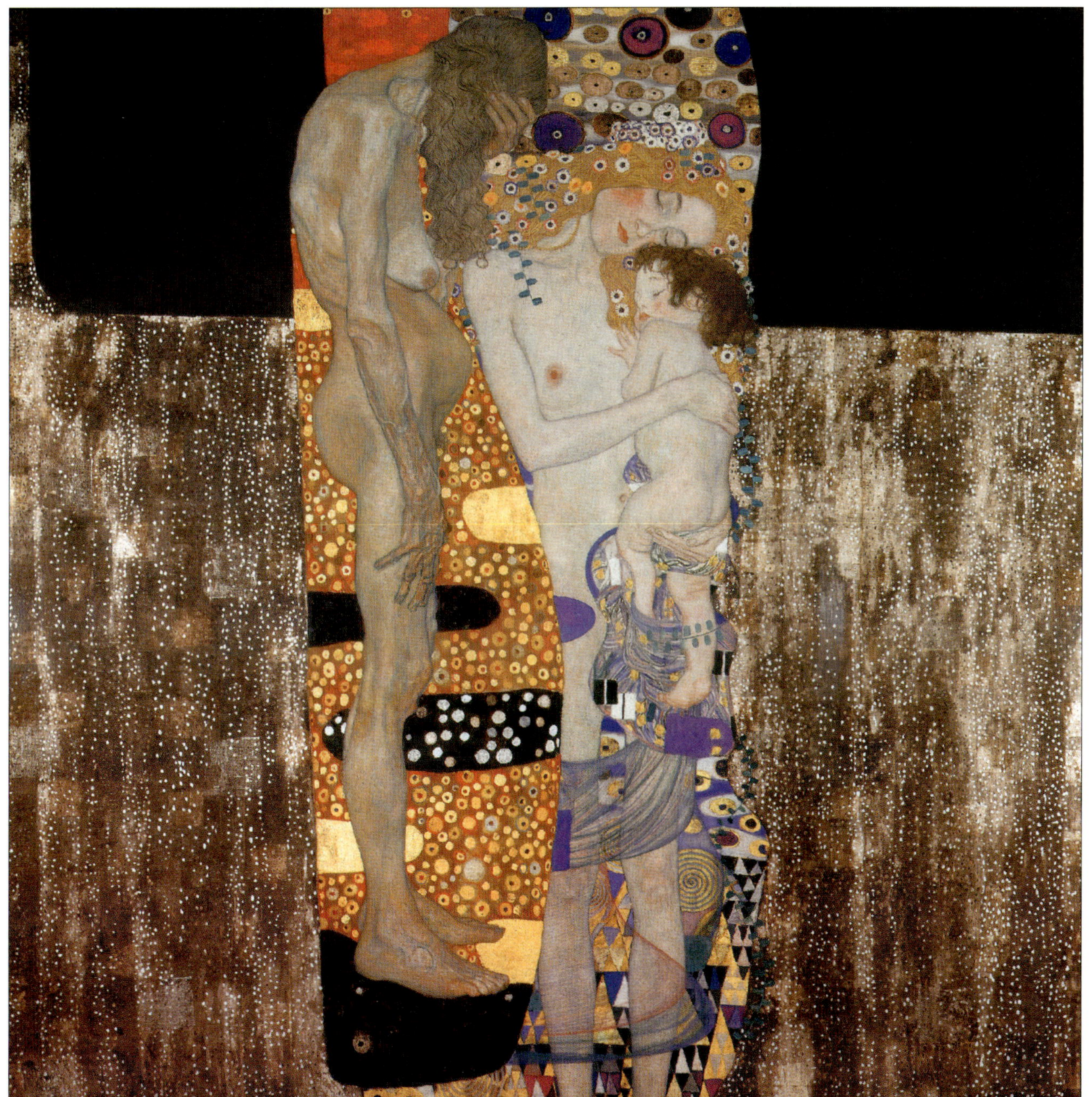

# PORTRAIT OF MARGARET STONBOROUGH–WITTGENSTEIN

*Oil on canvas. 1905. Neue Pinakothek, Bayerische Staatsgemäldesammlungen, Munich.*
*180 x 90.5 cm.*

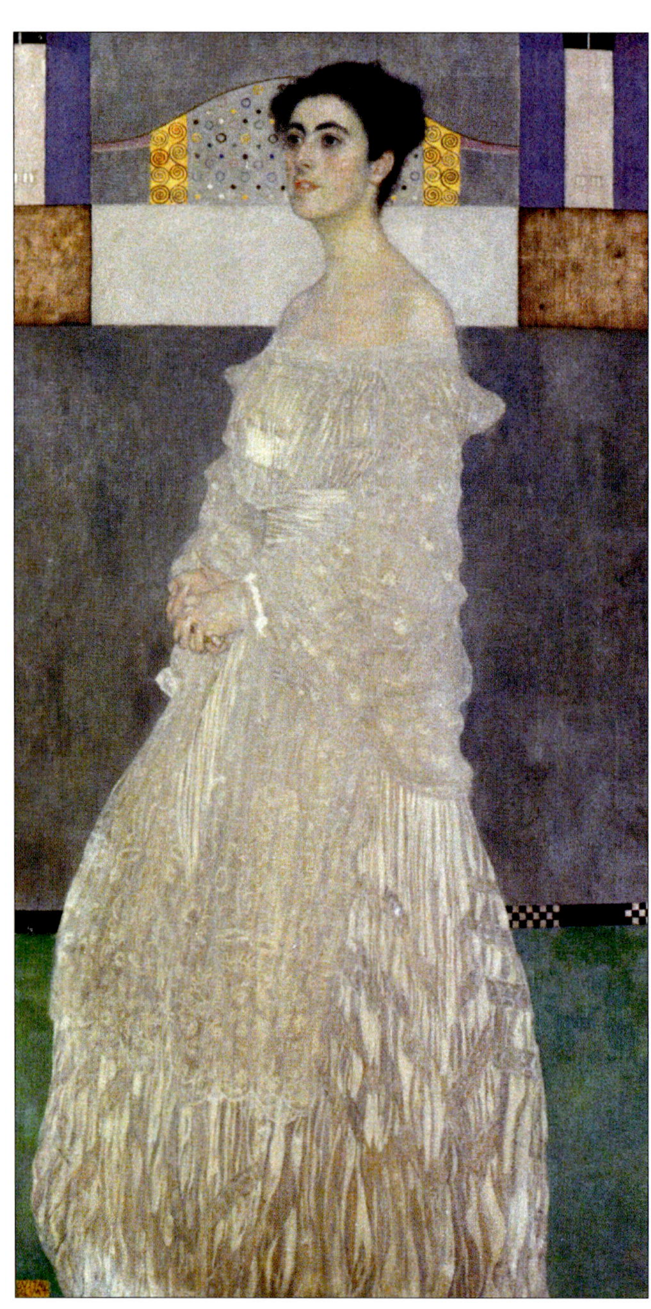

# FRITZA VON RIEDLER

*Oil on canvas. 1906. Österreichische Galerie Belvedere, Vienna, Austria.*
*153 x 133 cm.*

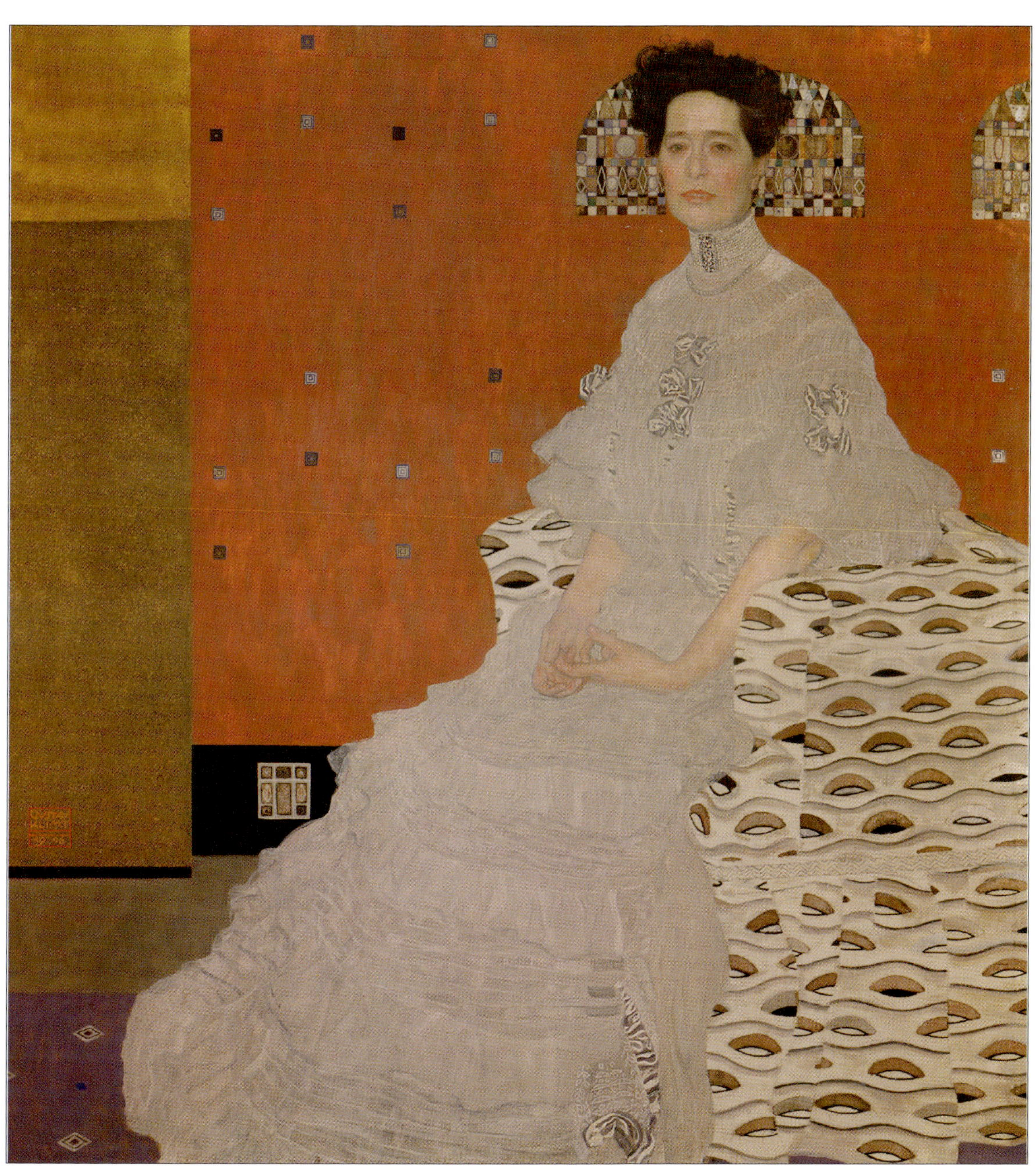

# FARM GARDEN WITH FLOWERS
## (BREWERY GARDEN AT LITZLBERG ON THE ATTERSEE)

*Oil on canvas. c.1906. Osterreichische Galerie Belvedere, Vienna, Austria. 110 x 110 cm.*

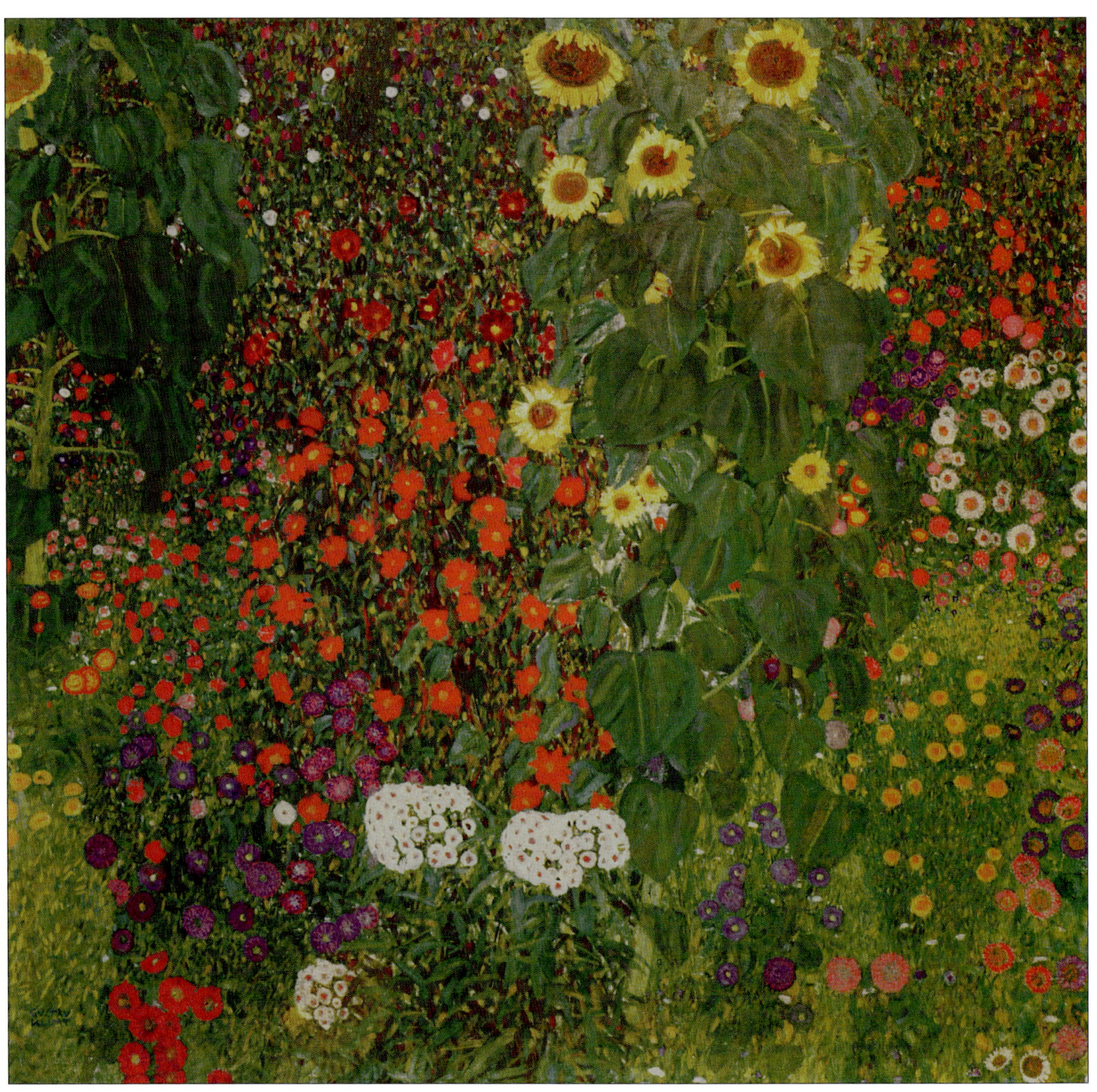

*Oil on canvas. 1907–08, Private collection. 77 x 83 cm.*

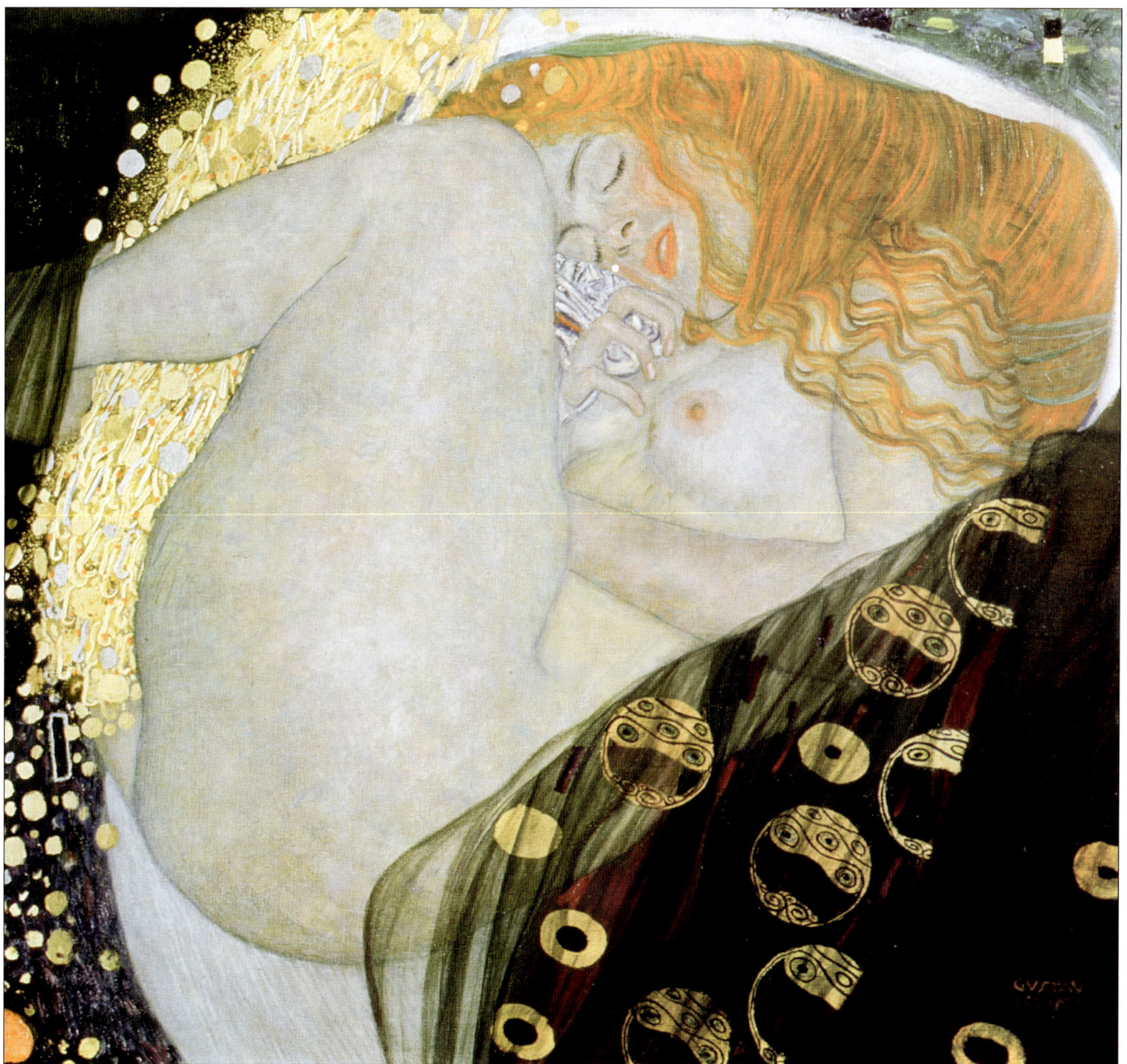

# THE KISS

*Oil on canvas. 1907–08. Osterreichische Galerie Belvedere, Vienna, Austria. 180 x 180 cm.*

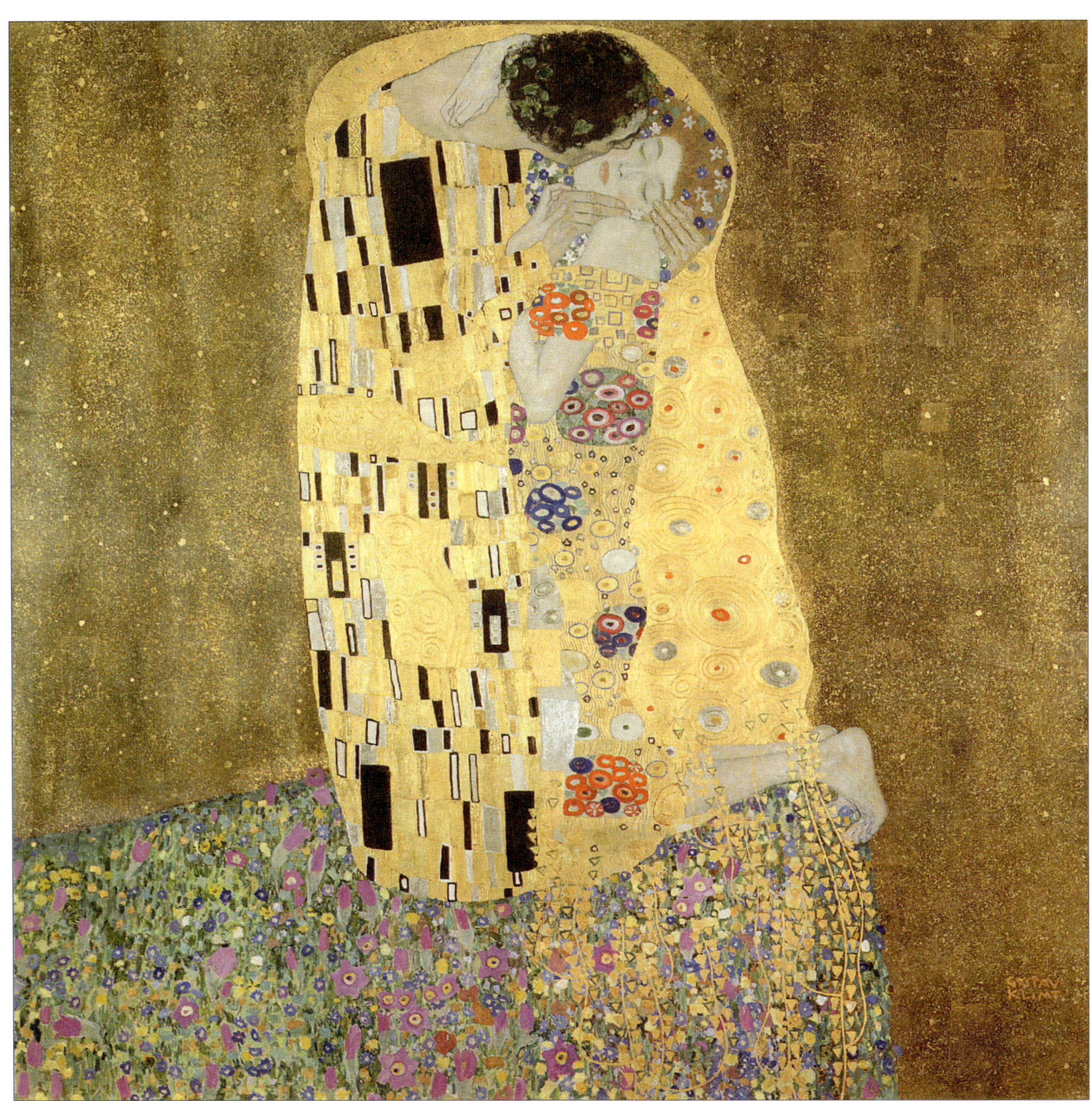

# ADELE BLOCH–BAUER I



*Oil on canvas. 1907. Neue Galerie, New York.*
*138 x 138 cm.*

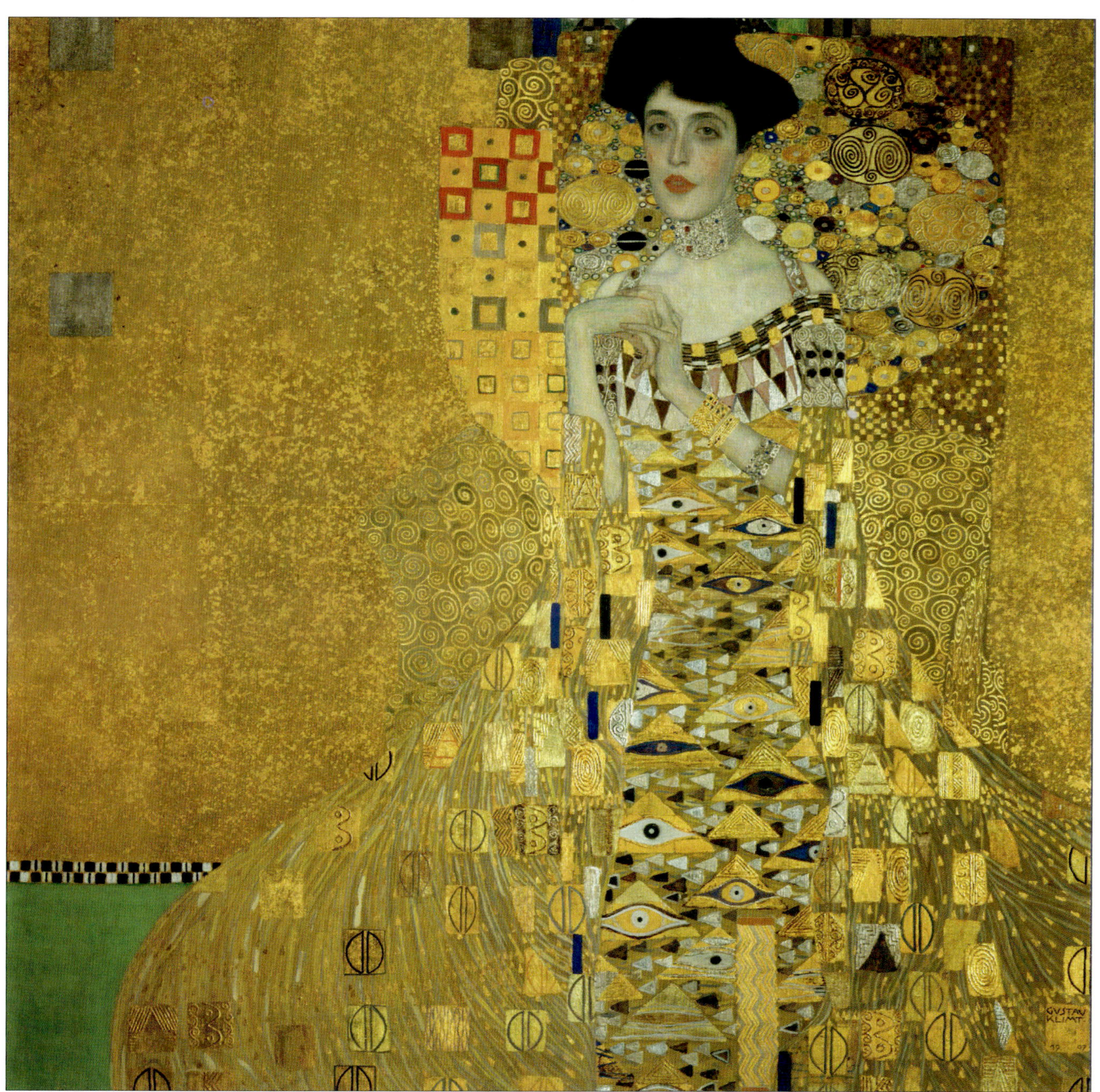

# DIE HOFFNUNG II (HOPE II)

*Oil and gold paint on canvas. 1907–8. Museum of Modern Art, New York. 110 x 110 cm.*

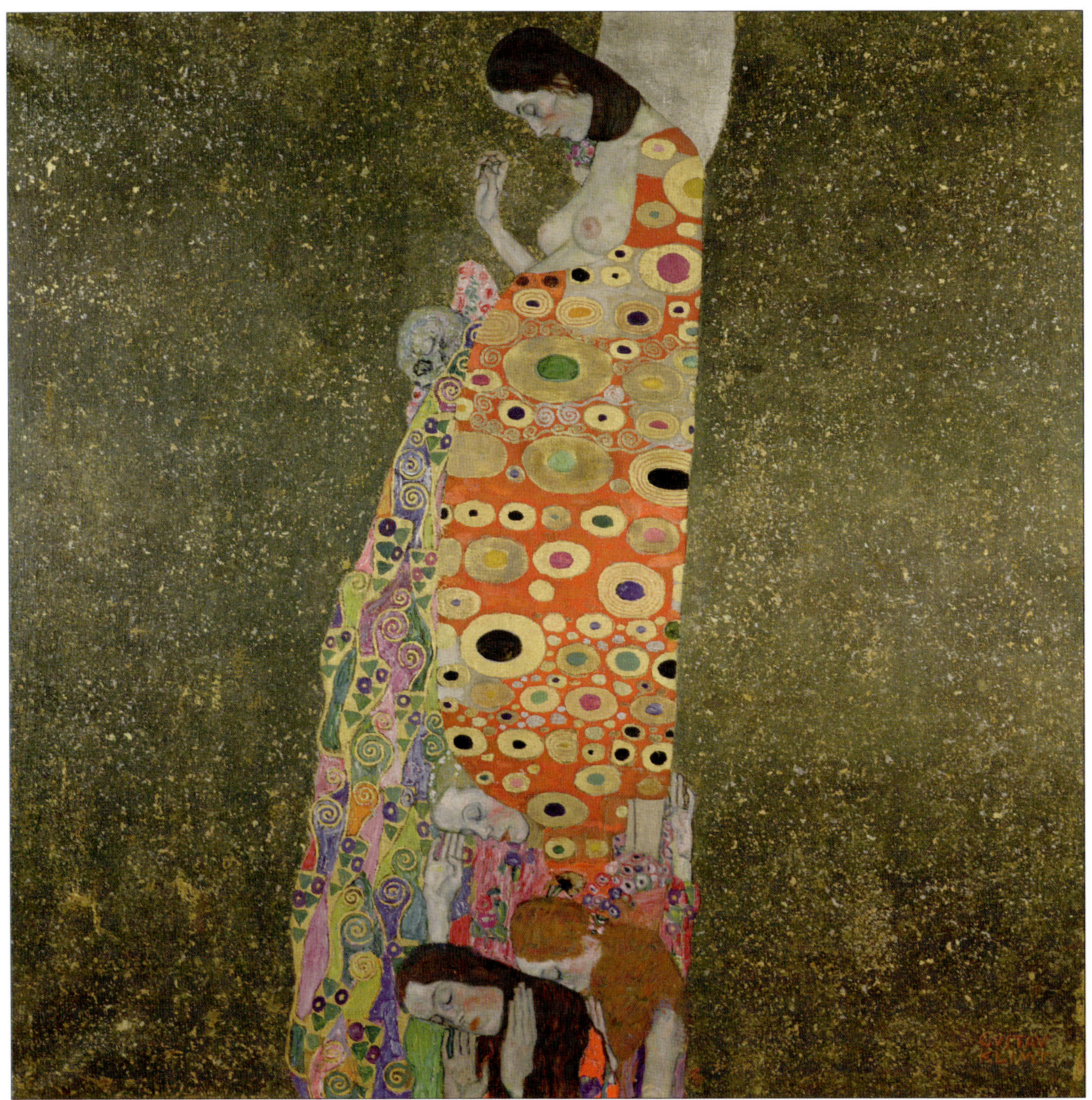

# SCHLOSS KAMMER AM ATTERSEE II

*Oil on cardboard. c.1909. Private collection. 110 x 110 cm.*

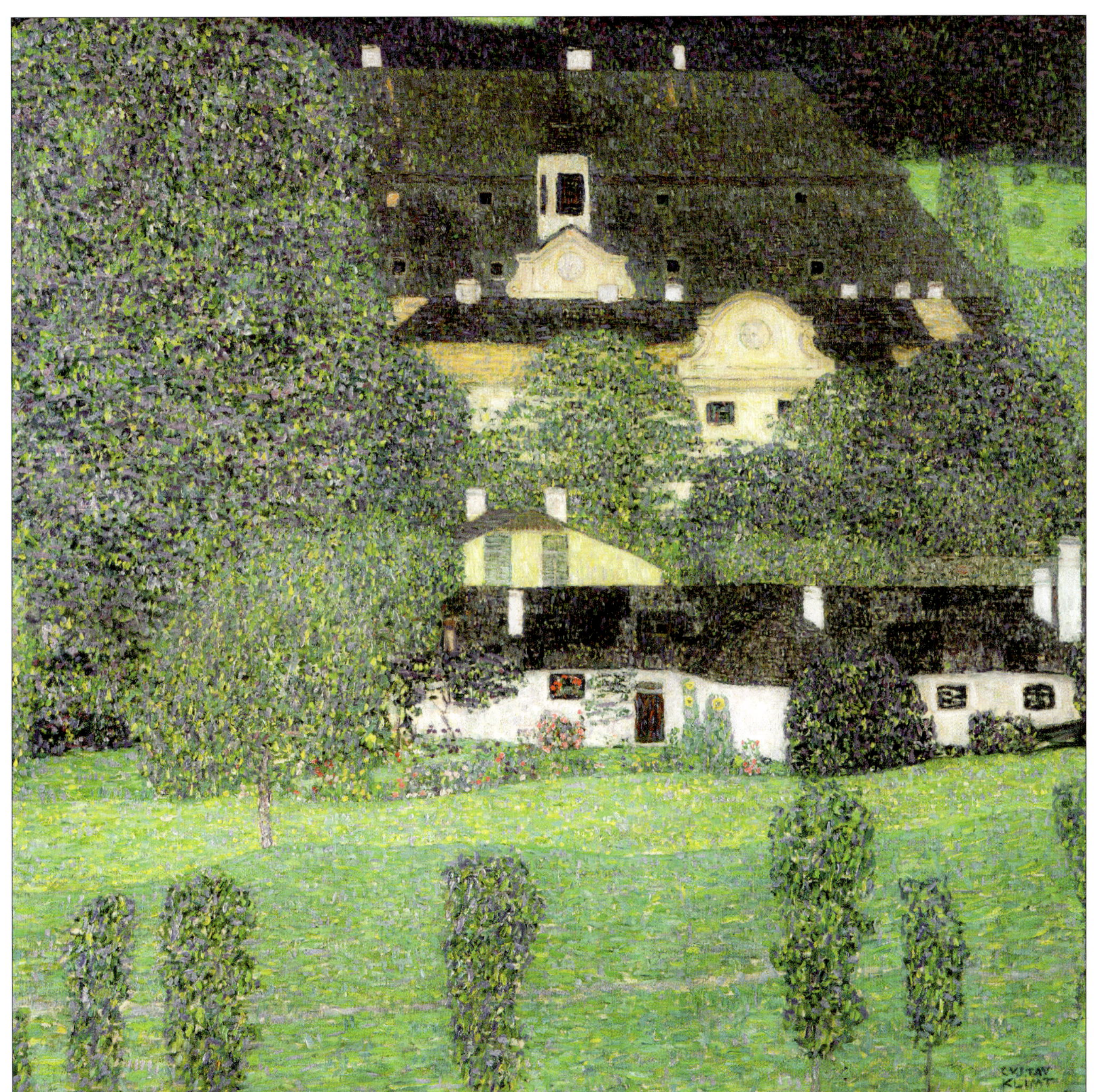

# JUDITH II (SALOME)

*Oil on canvas. 1909. Museo d'Arte Moderna, Venice, Italy. 178 x 46 cm.*

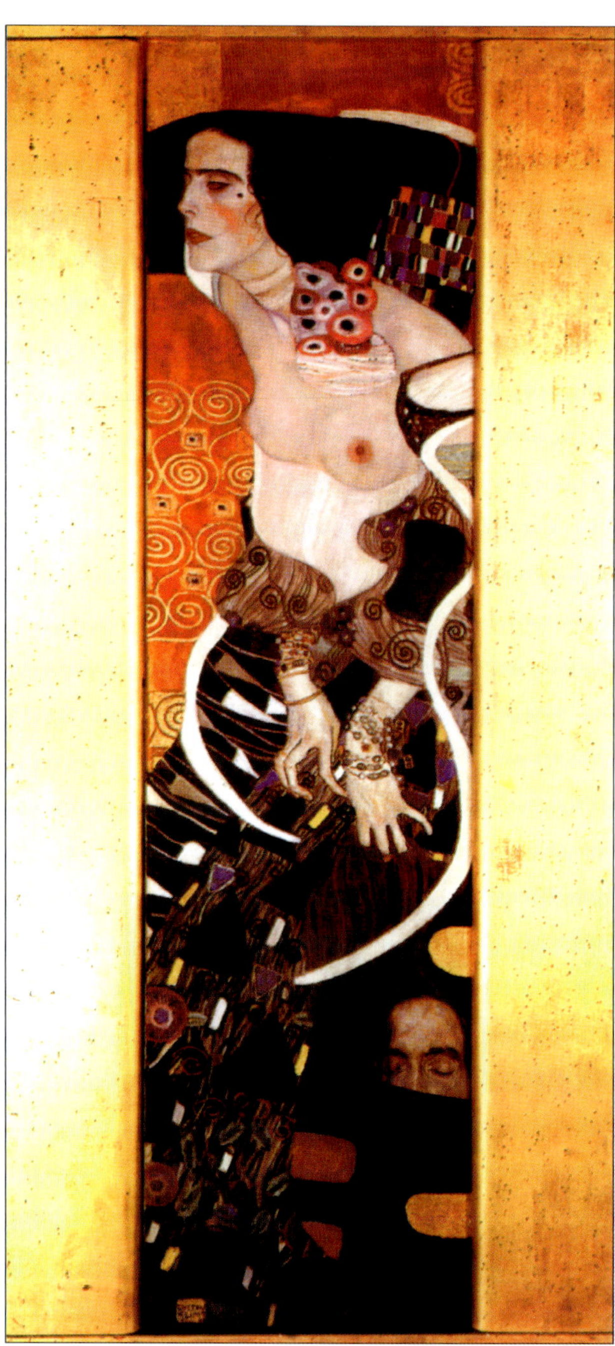

*Oil on canvas. 1909. Österreichische Galerie Belvedere, Vienna, Austria. 69 x 55 cm.*

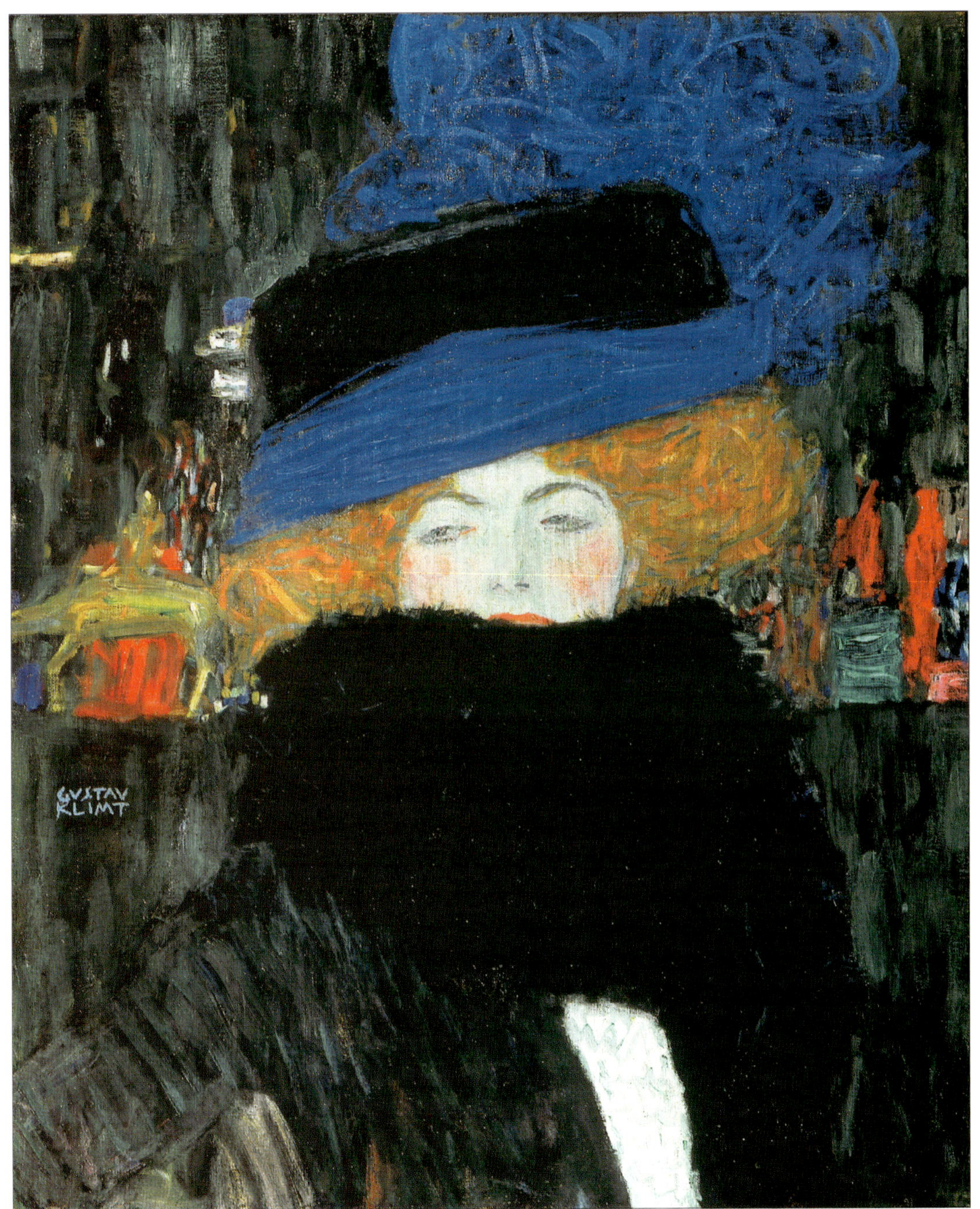

# GIRL IN WHITE

*Oil on canvas. c.1910. Osterreichische Galerie Belvedere, Vienna, Austria. 150 x 110 cm.*

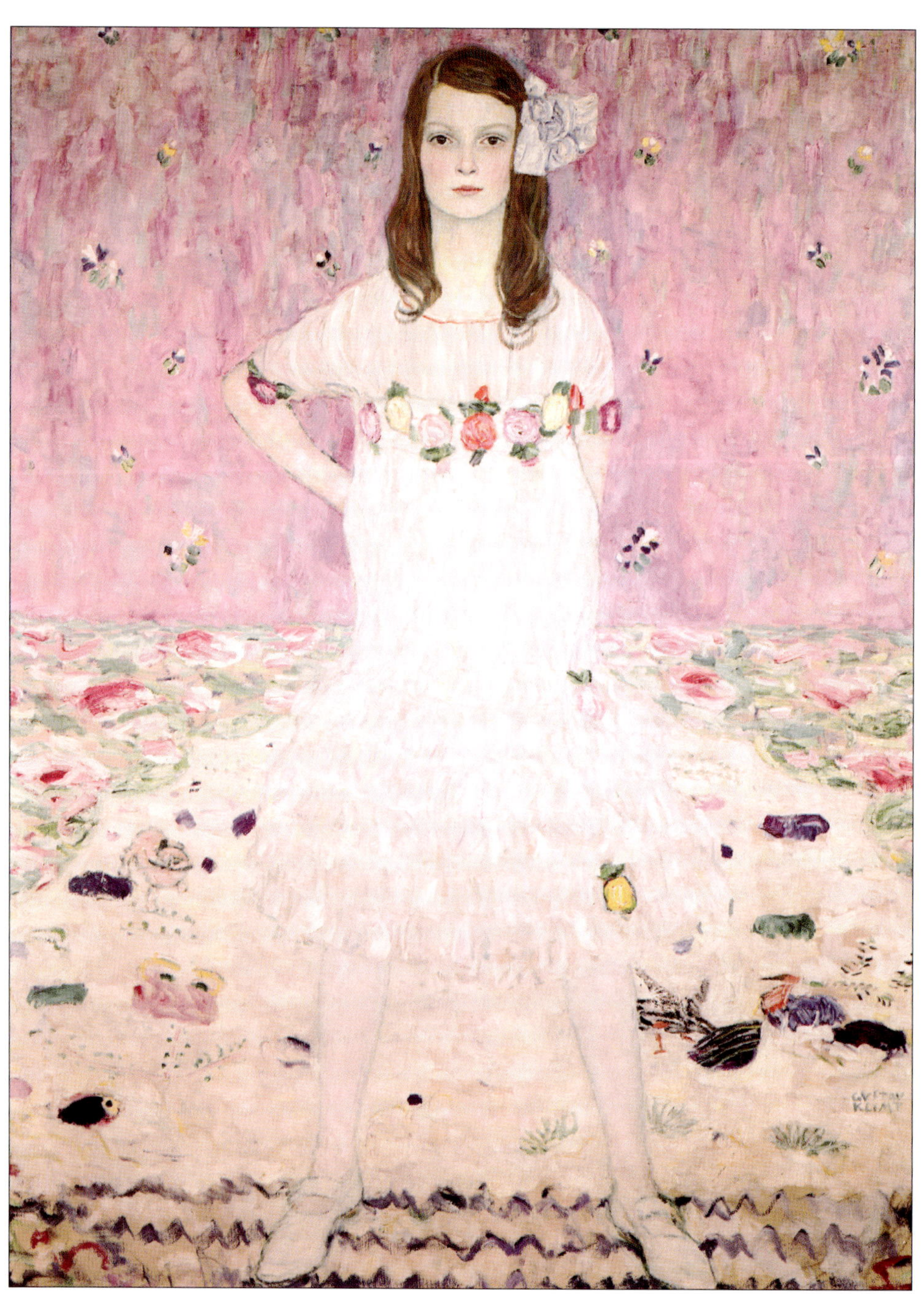

*Oil on canvas. 1910. Private collection. 110 x 110 cm.*

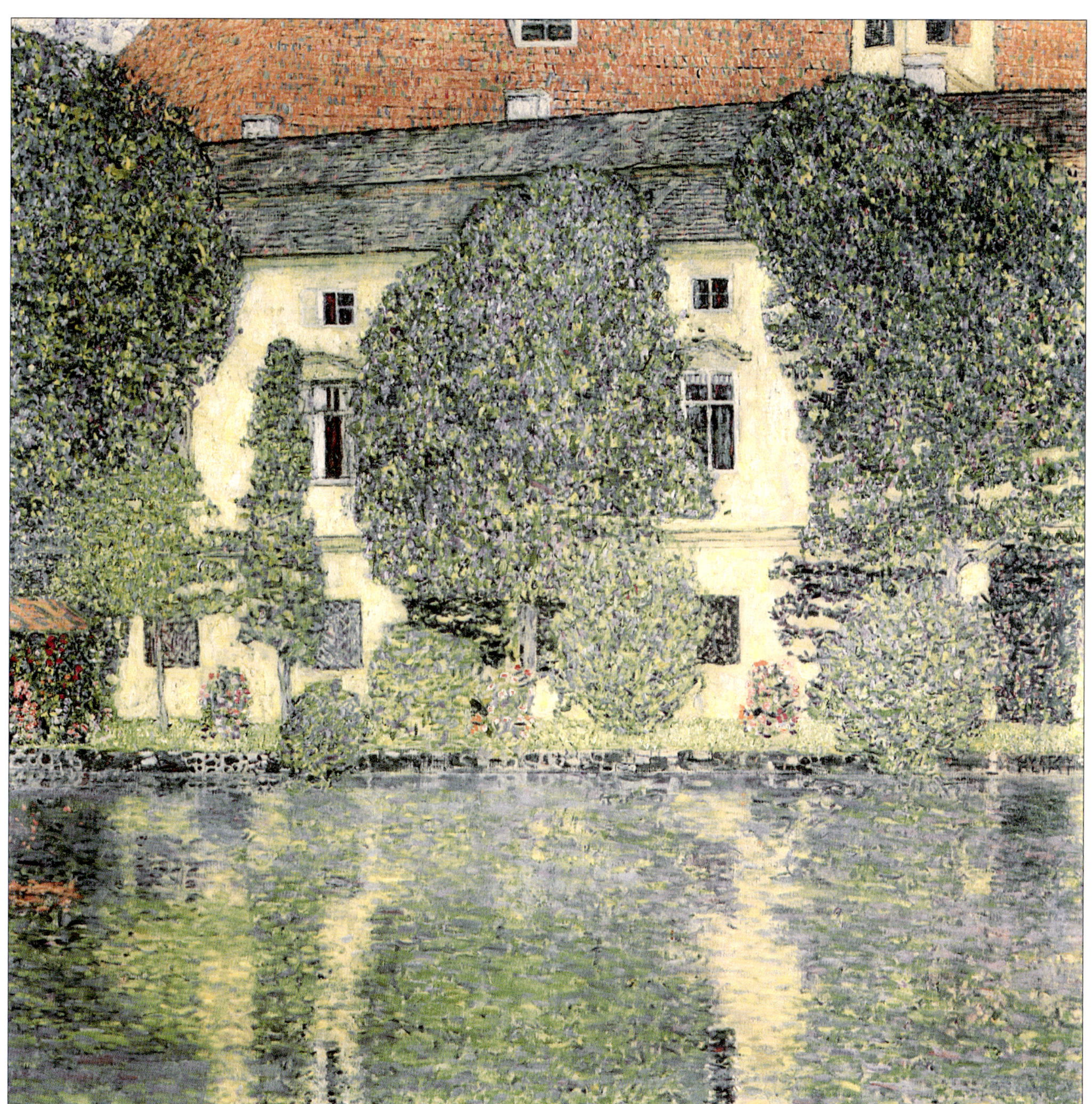

# ORCHARD WITH ROSES

*Oil on canvas. 1911–12. Private collection. 110 x 110 cm.*

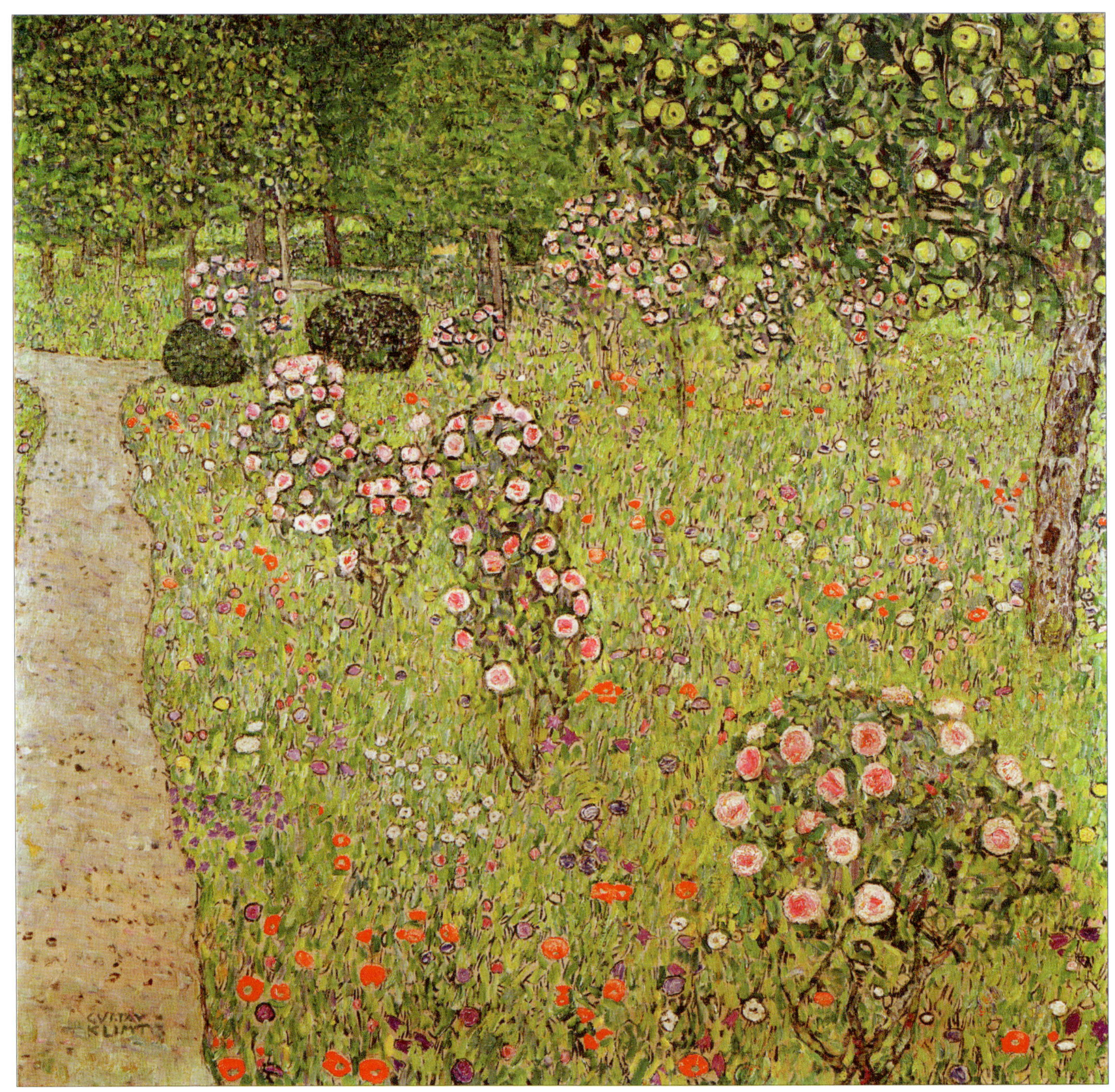

*Oil on canvas. 1912. Private collection. 110 x 110 cm.*

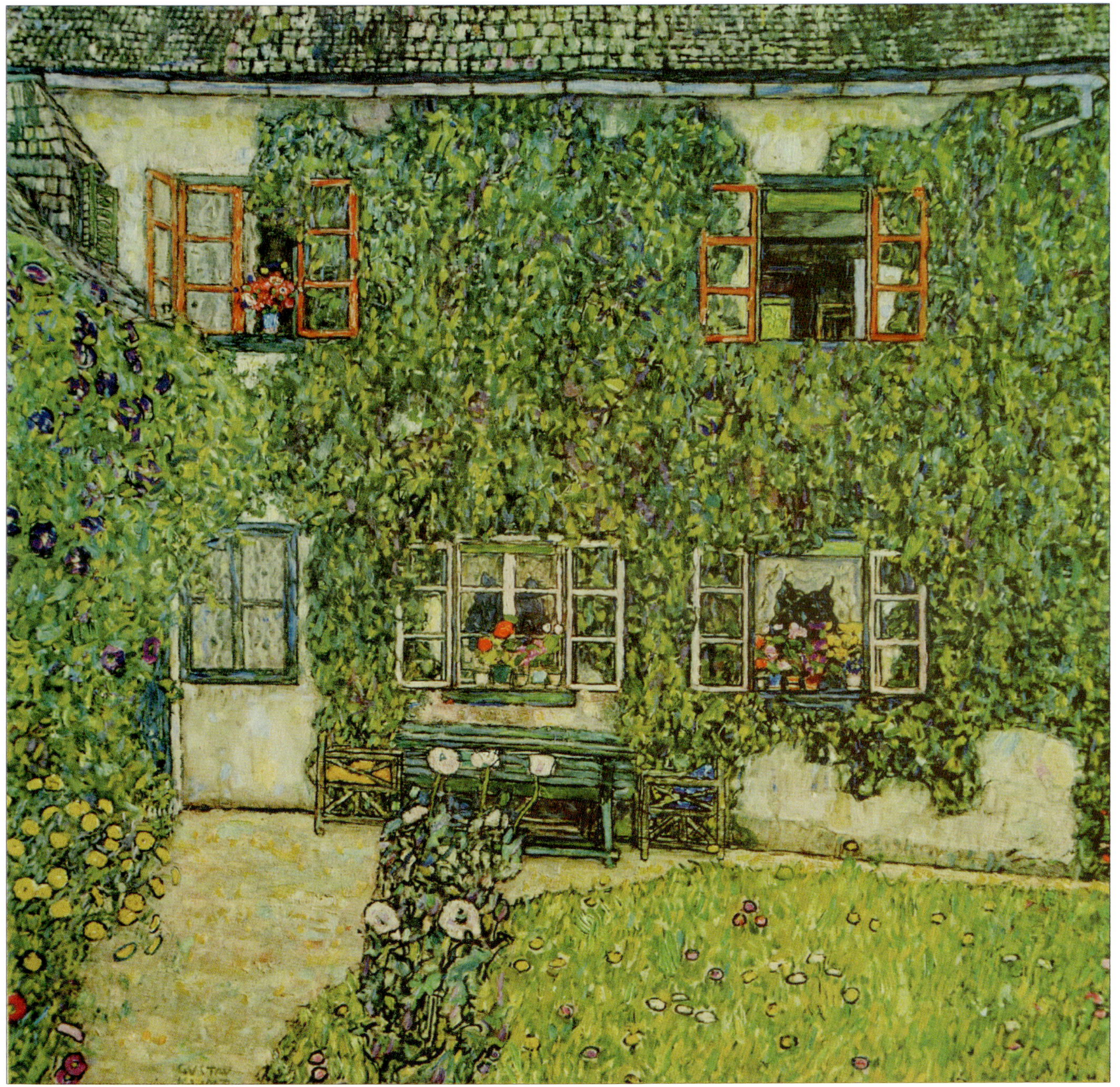

# AVENUE IN SCHLOSS KAMMER PARK

*Oil on canvas. 1912. Österreichische Galerie Belvedere, Vienna, Austria.*
*110 x 110 cm.*

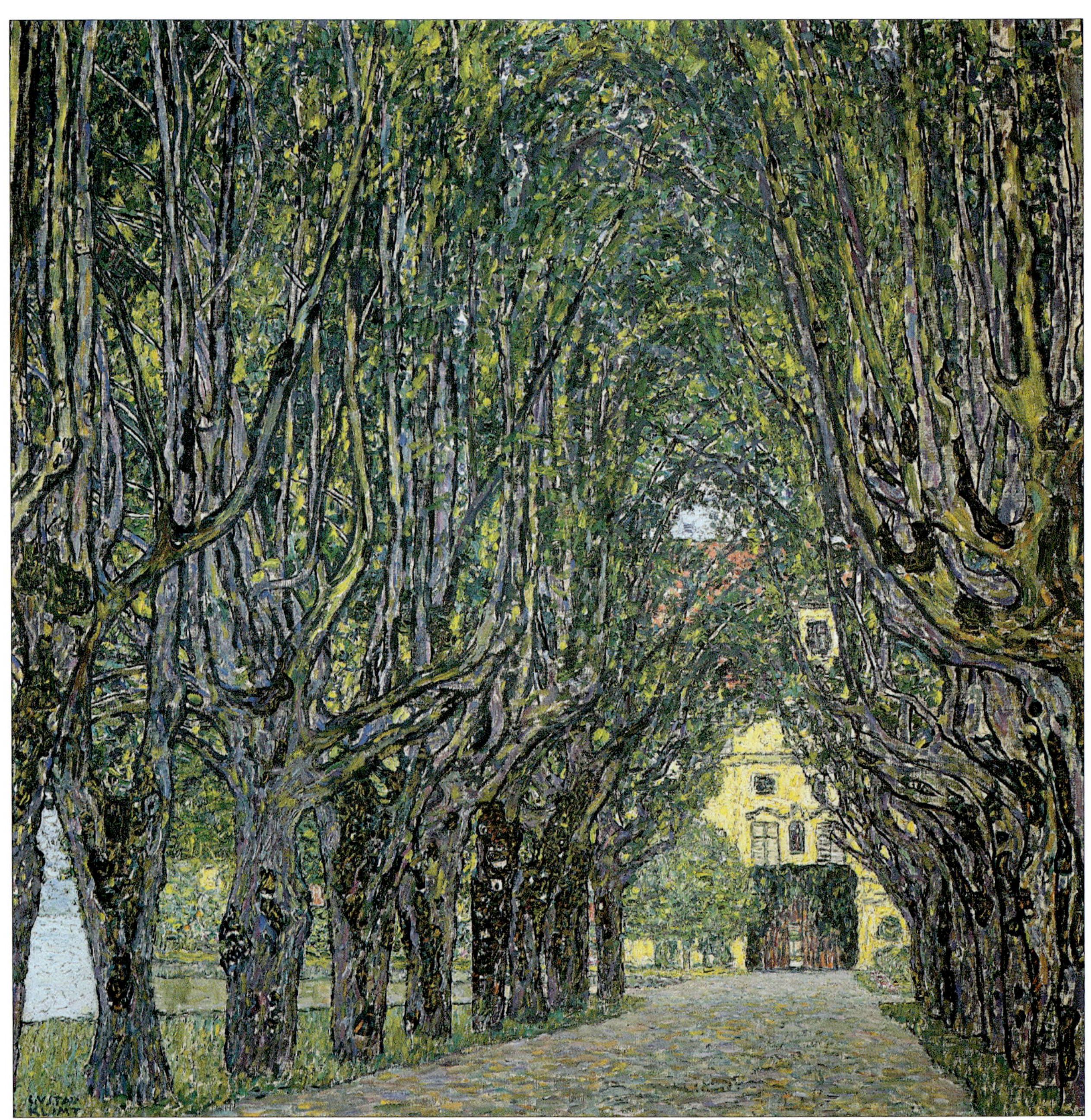

# ADELE BLOCH–BAUER II

*Oil on canvas. 1912. Private collection. 190 x 120 cm.*

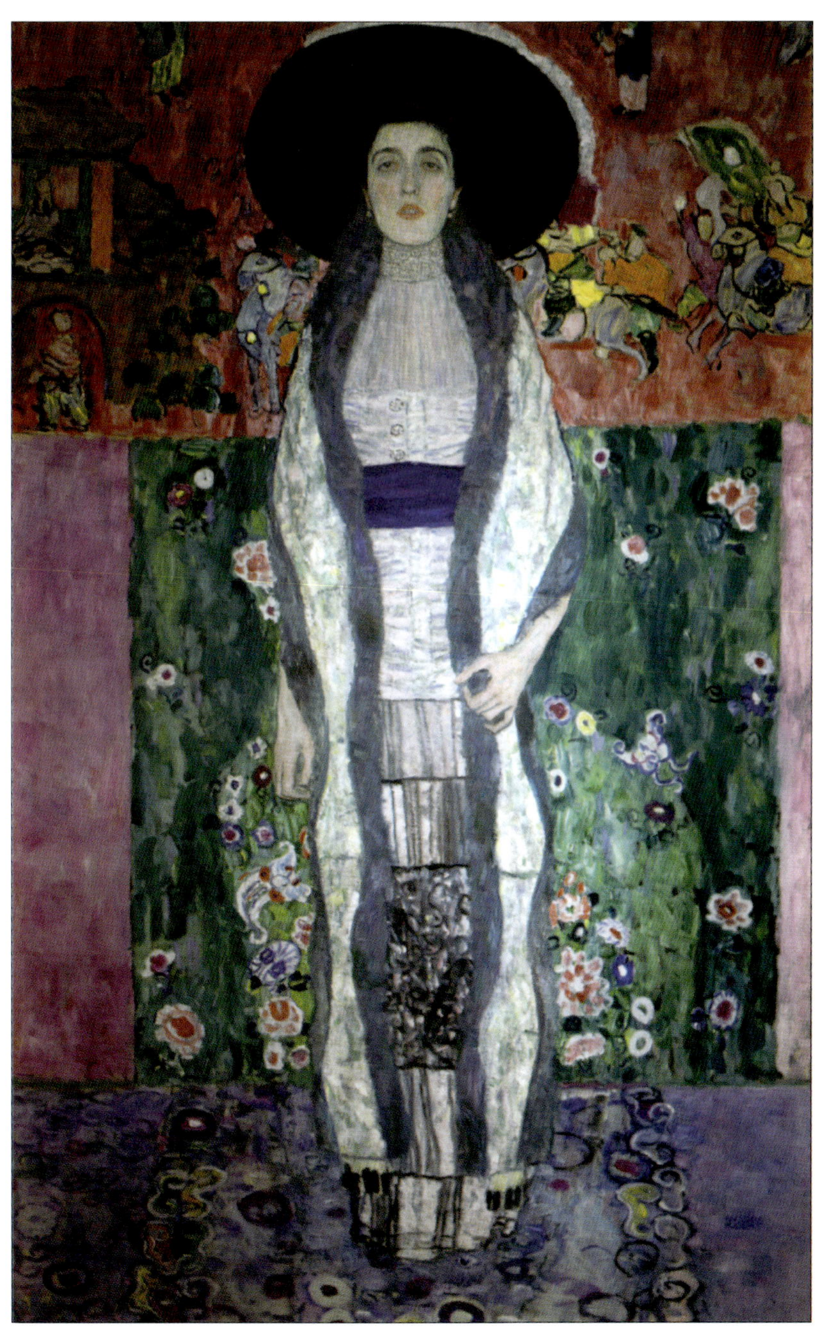

# DEATH AND LIFE

*Oil on canvas. c.1911. Private collection. 178 x 198 cm.*

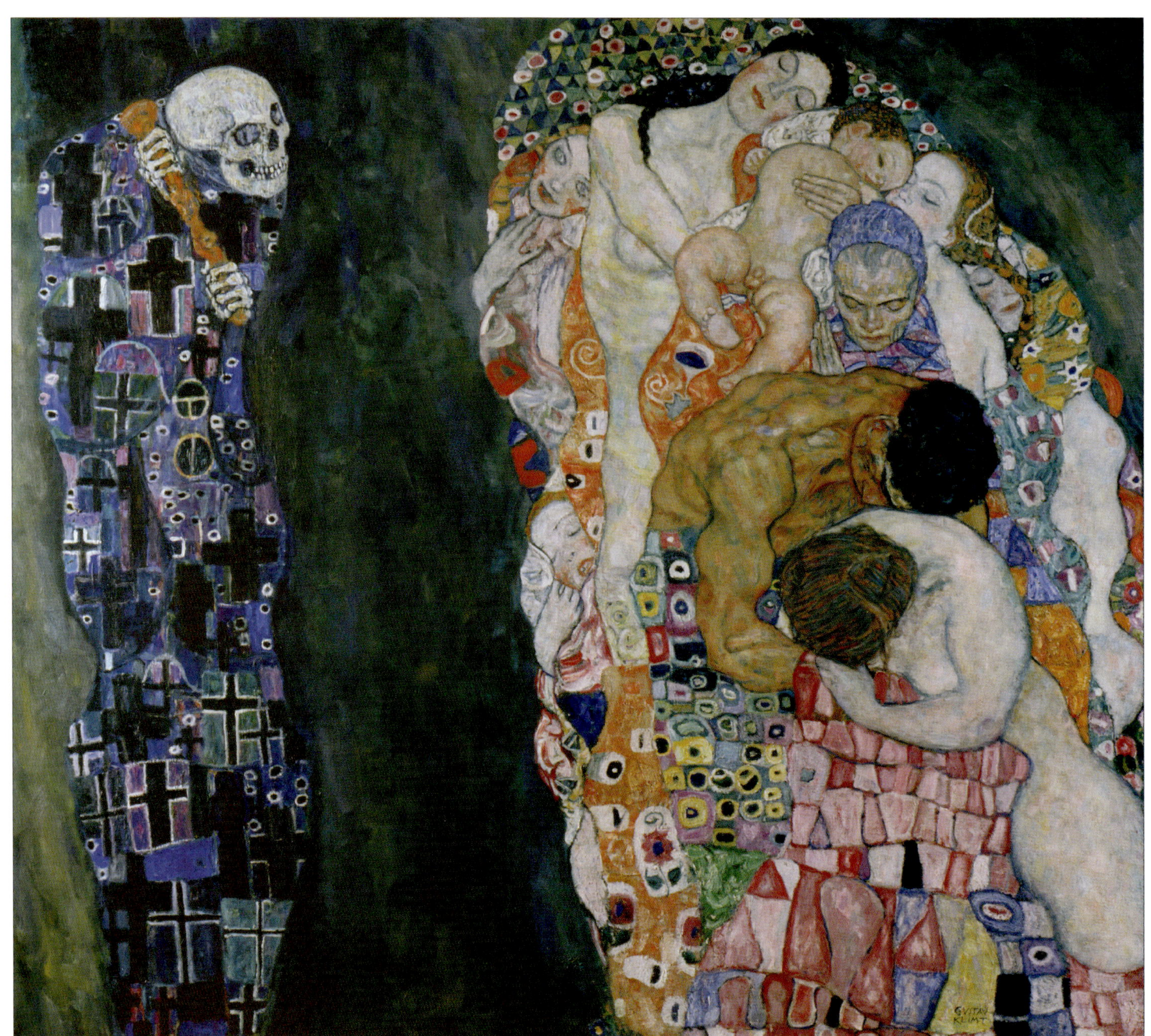

*Oil on canvas. 1913. Národní Galerie, Prague, Czech Republic. 190 x 200 cm.*

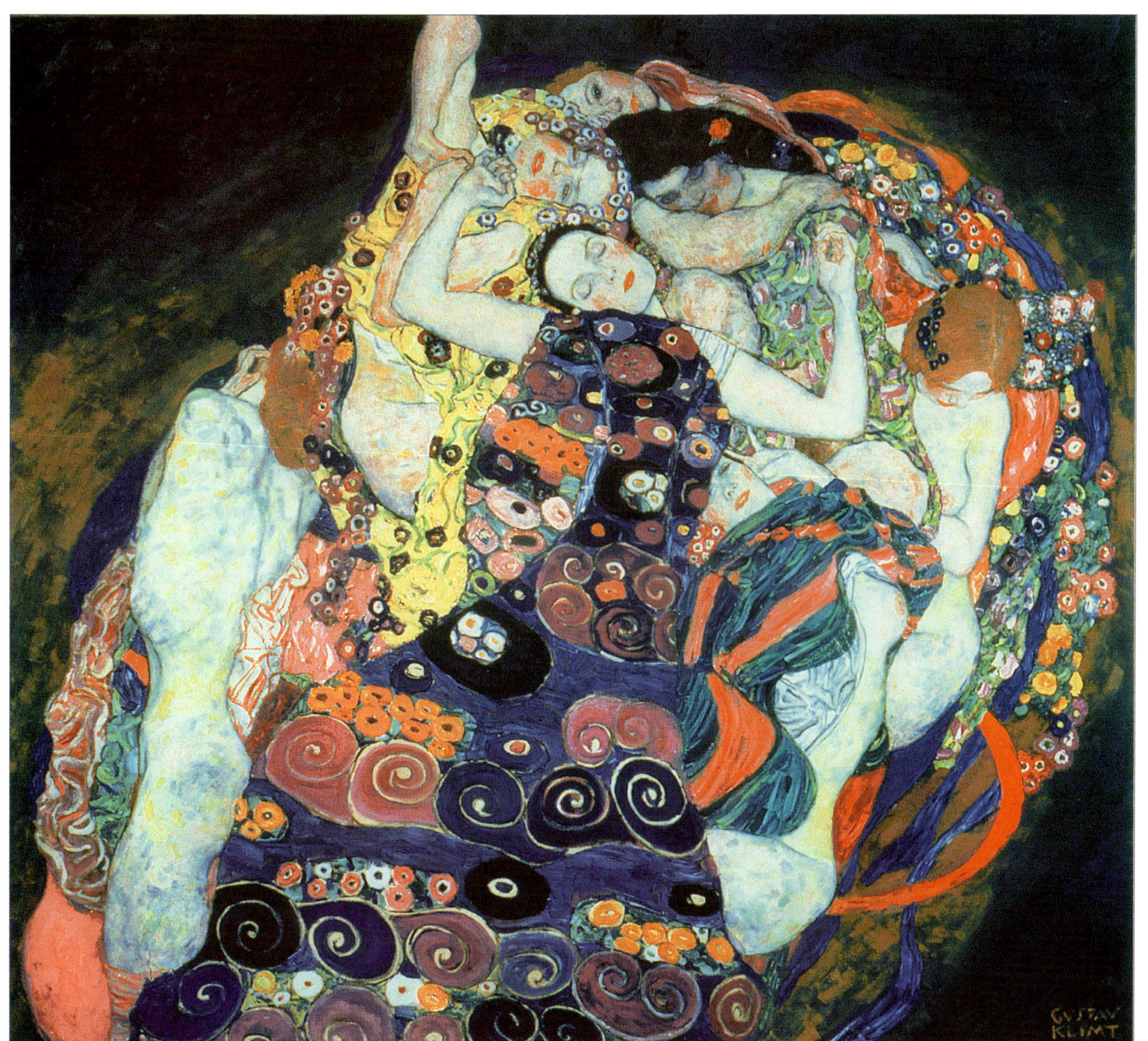

# IMAGE OF EUGENIA PRIMAVESI

*Oil on canvas. c.1913. Toyota Municipal Museum of Art, Toyota, Japan. 140 x 85 cm.*

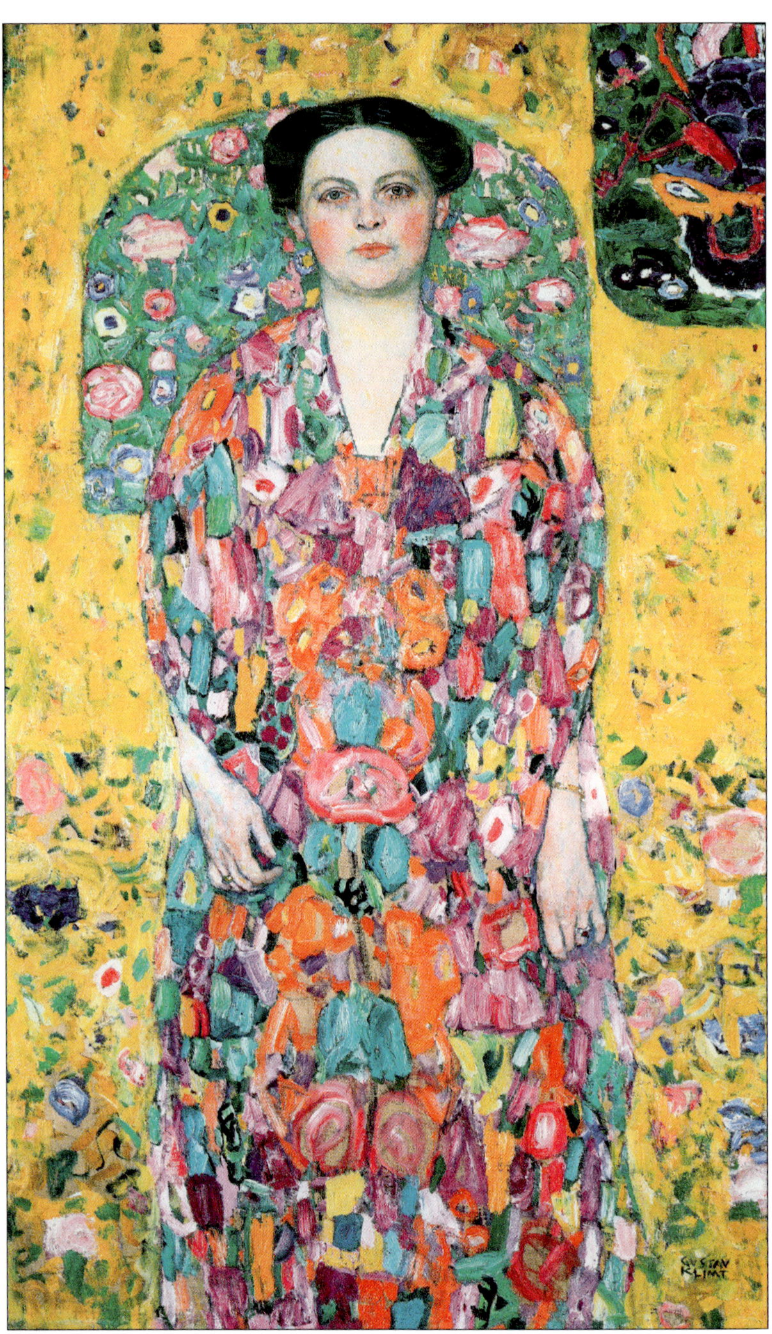

*Oil on canvas. 1914. Private collection. 180 x 128 cm.*

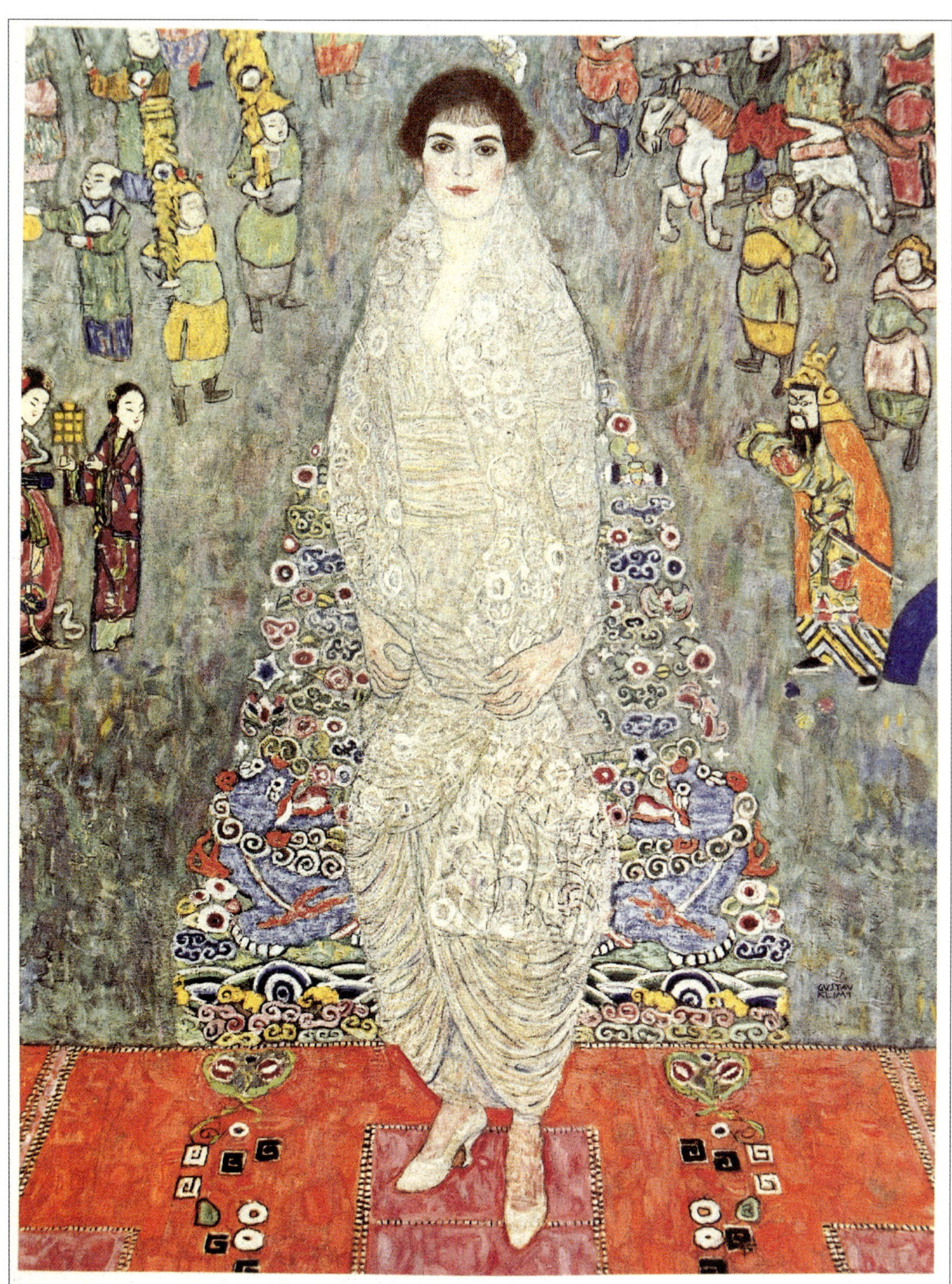

# COUNTRY HOUSE BY THE ATTERSEE
*Oil on canvas. c.1914. Private collection. 110 x 110 cm.*

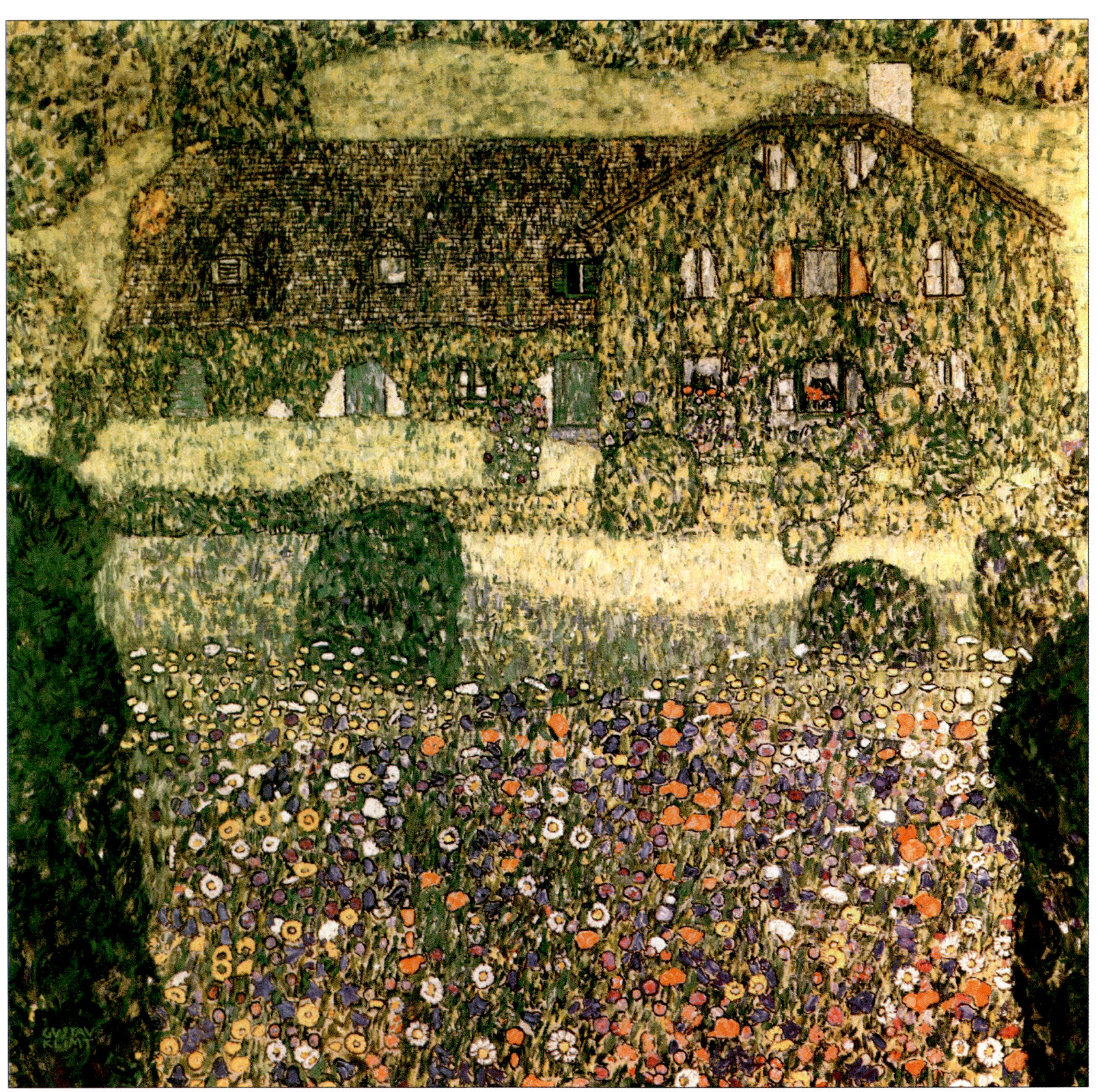

# UNTERACH AT THE ATTERSEE LAKE

*Oil on canvas. 1915. Museum der Moderne, Salzburg. 111 x 111 cm.*

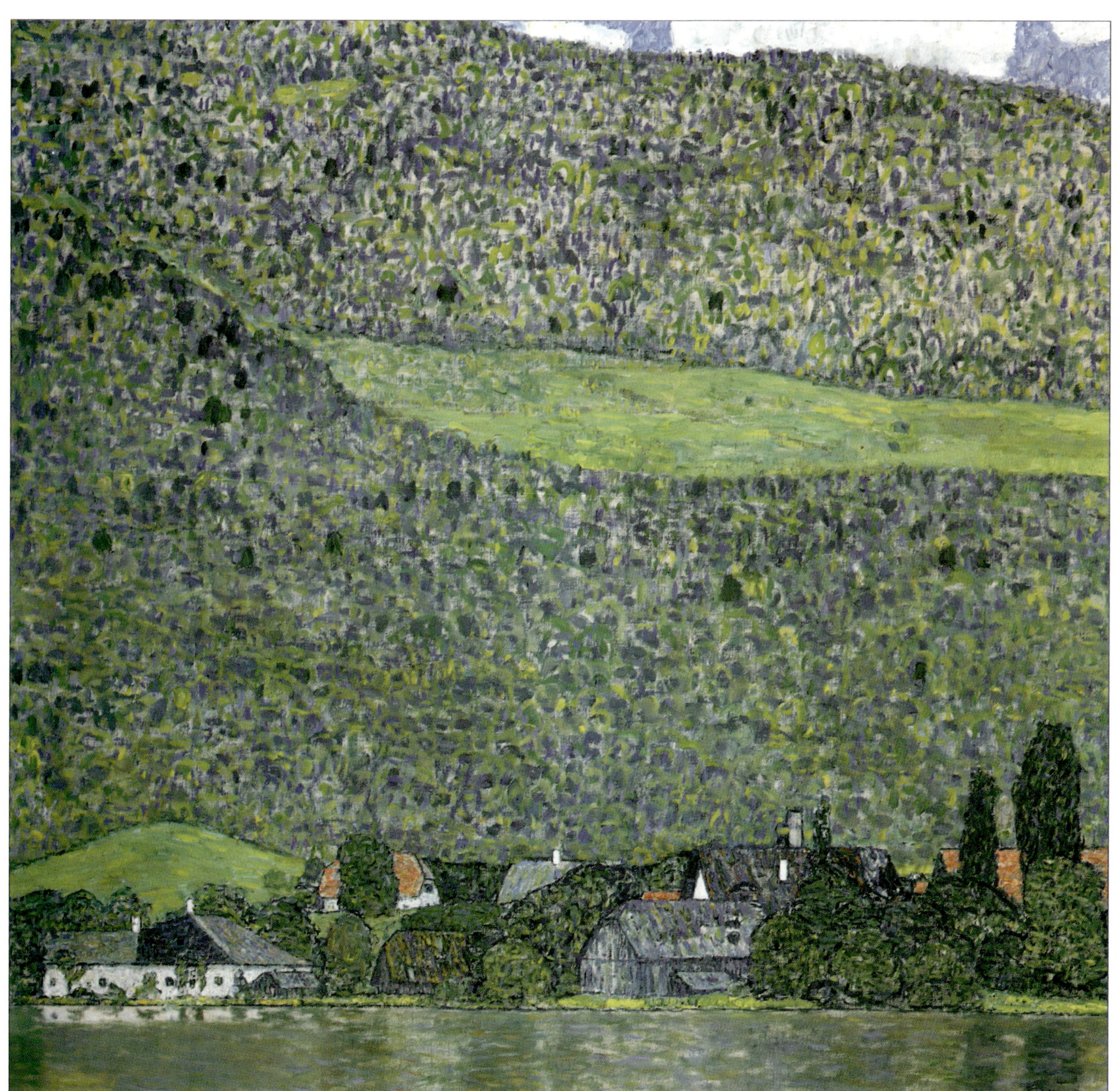

# THE APPLE TREE II

*Oil on canvas. 1916. Private collection. 80 x 80 cm.*

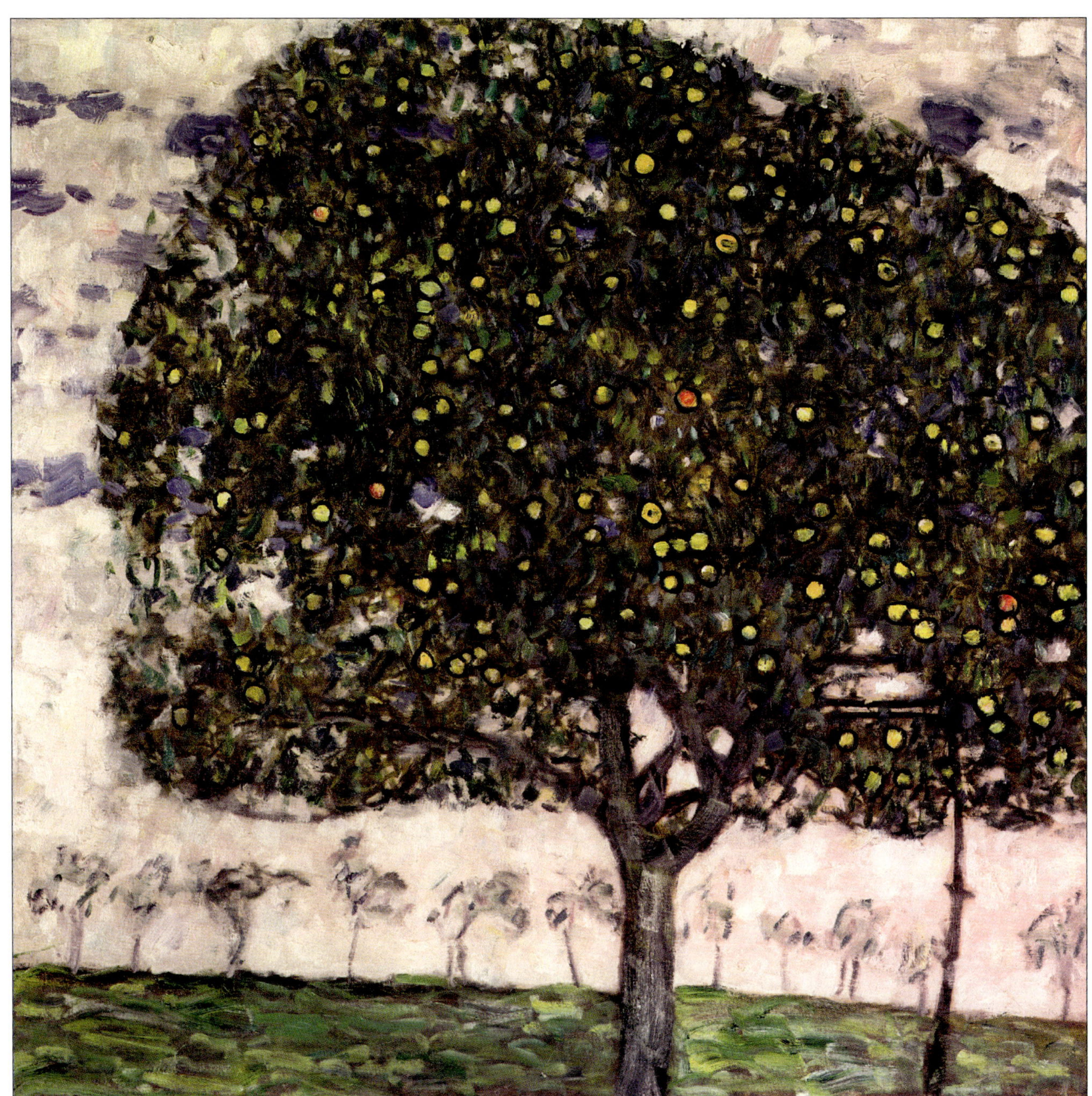

*Oil on canvas. 1917. Private collection.*
*110 x 110 cm.*

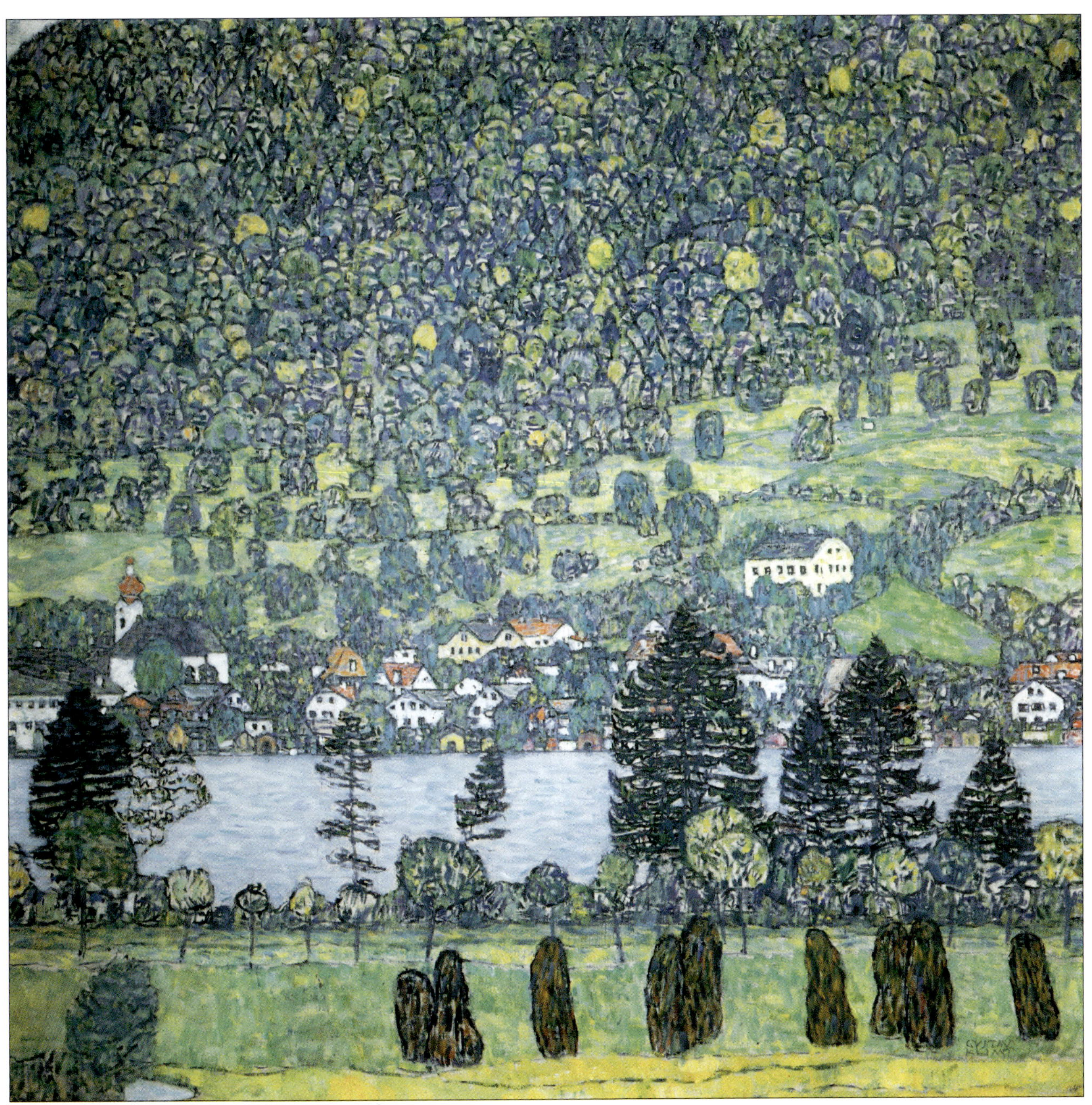

# PORTRAIT OF FRIEDERIKE BEER

*Oil on canvas. 1916. Private collection.*
*168 x 130 cm.*

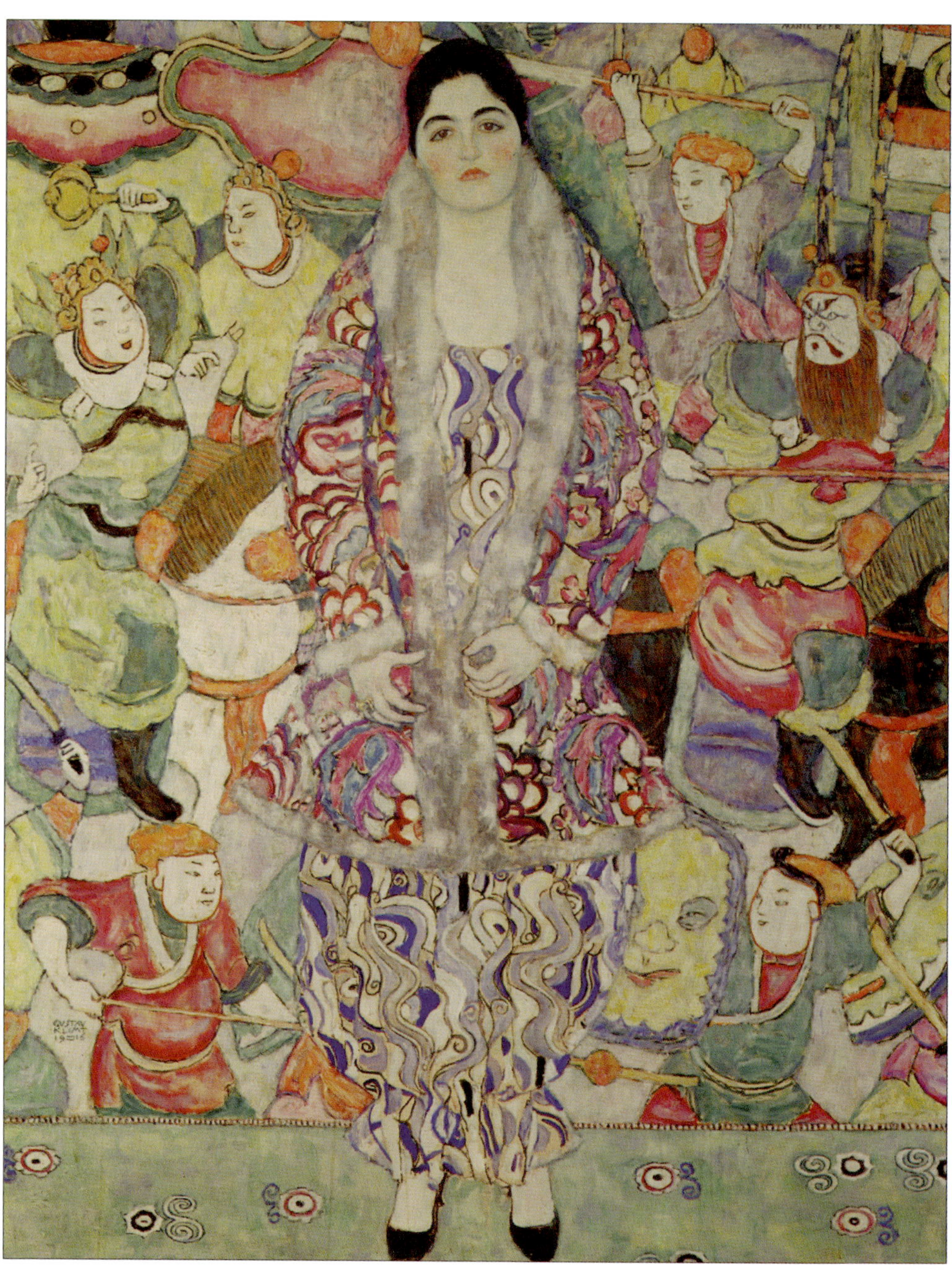

# WOMEN FRIENDS

*Oil on canvas. 1916–17. Destroyed in 1945.*
*Österreichische Galerie Belvedere, Vienna, Austria. 99 x 99 cm.*

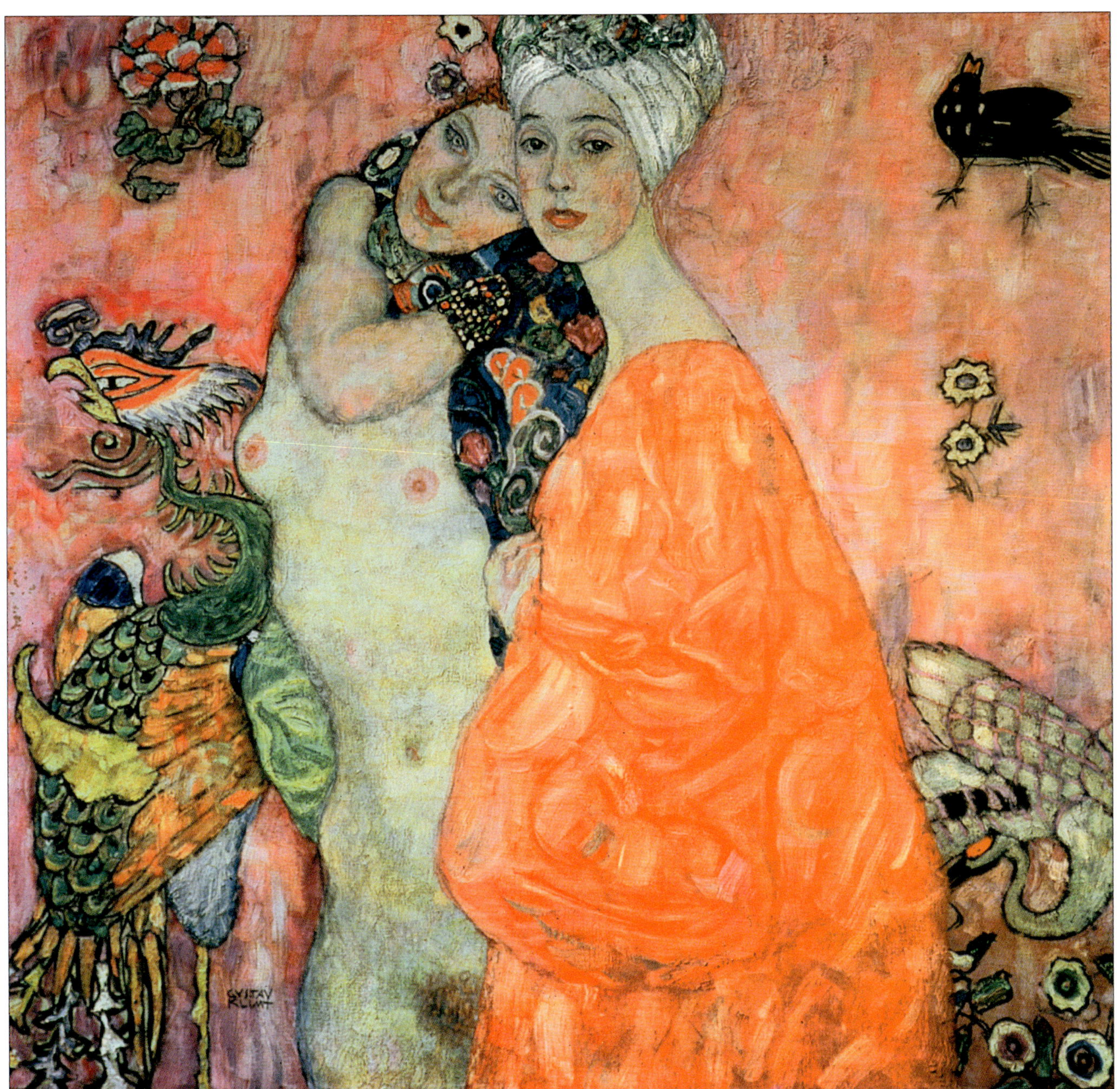

# PORTRAIT OF A LADY

*Oil on canvas. 1916–17. Galleria Ricci Oddi, Piacenza.*
*60 x 55 cm.*

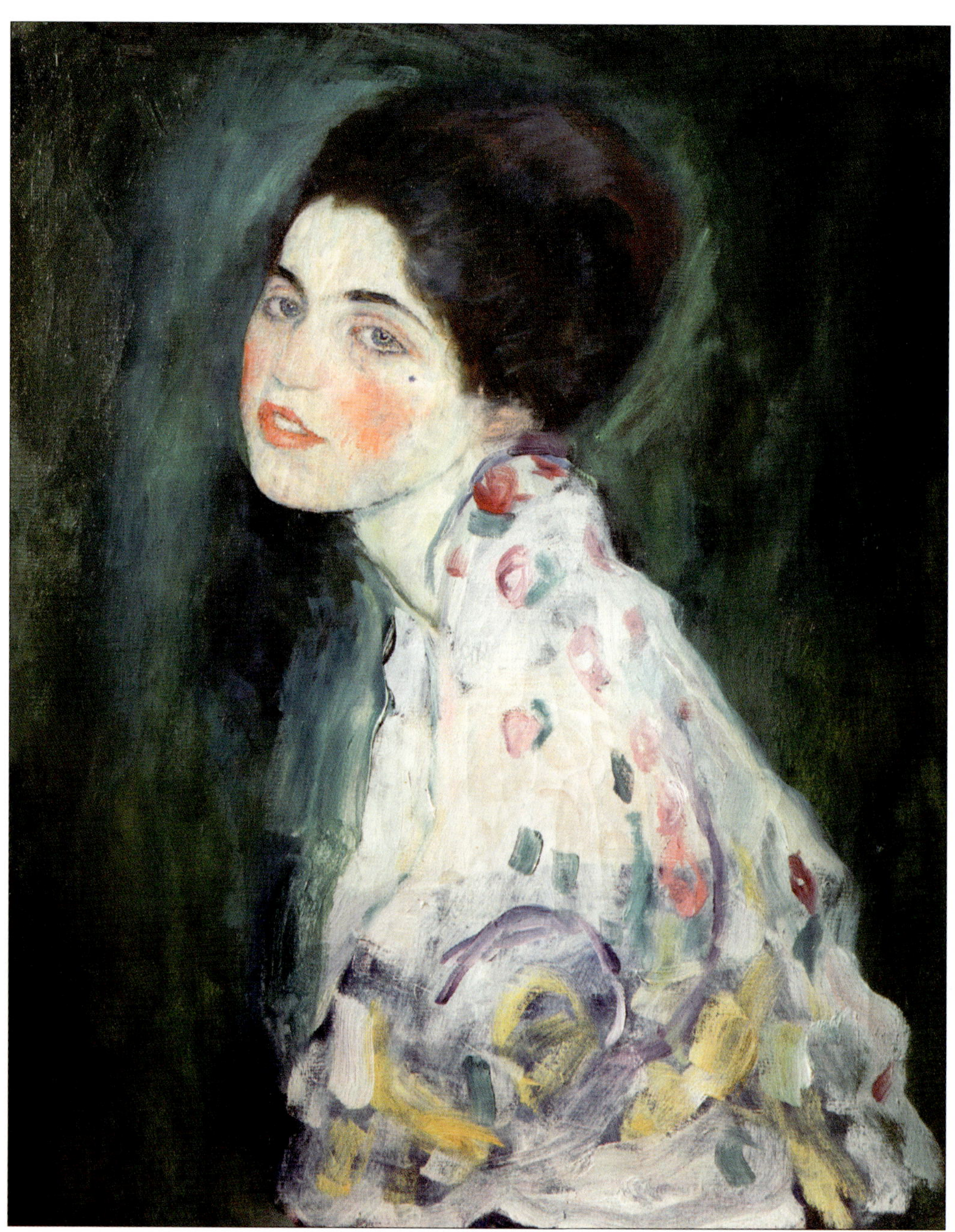

*Pen and ink and watercolour on paper. Unfinished 1917–18.*
*Neue Galerie, Linz, Austria. 67 x 56 cm.*

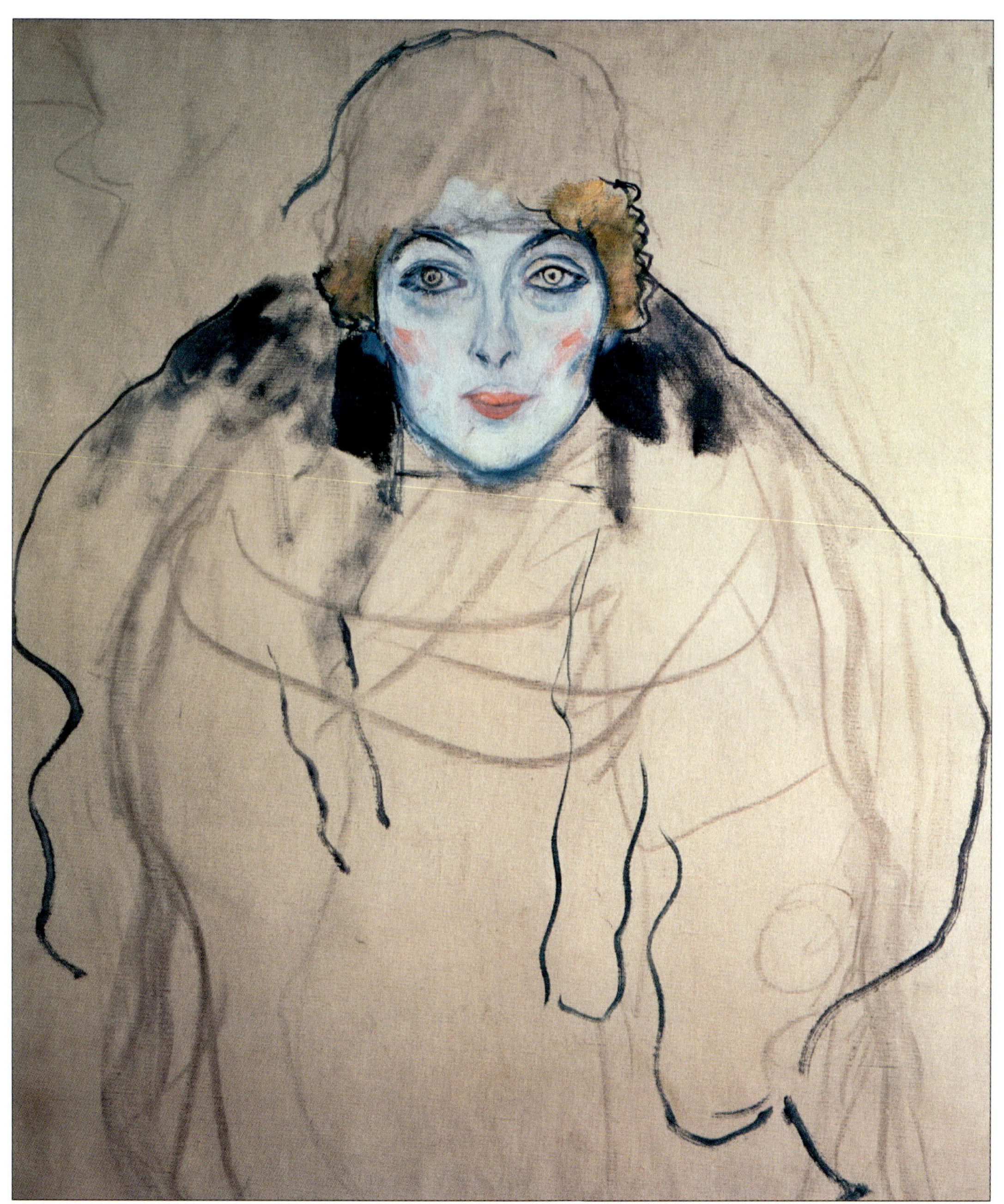

# LADY WITH FAN

*Oil on canvas. 1917–18. Galleria Nazionale d'Arte Moderna, Rome, Italy.*
*100 x 100 cm.*

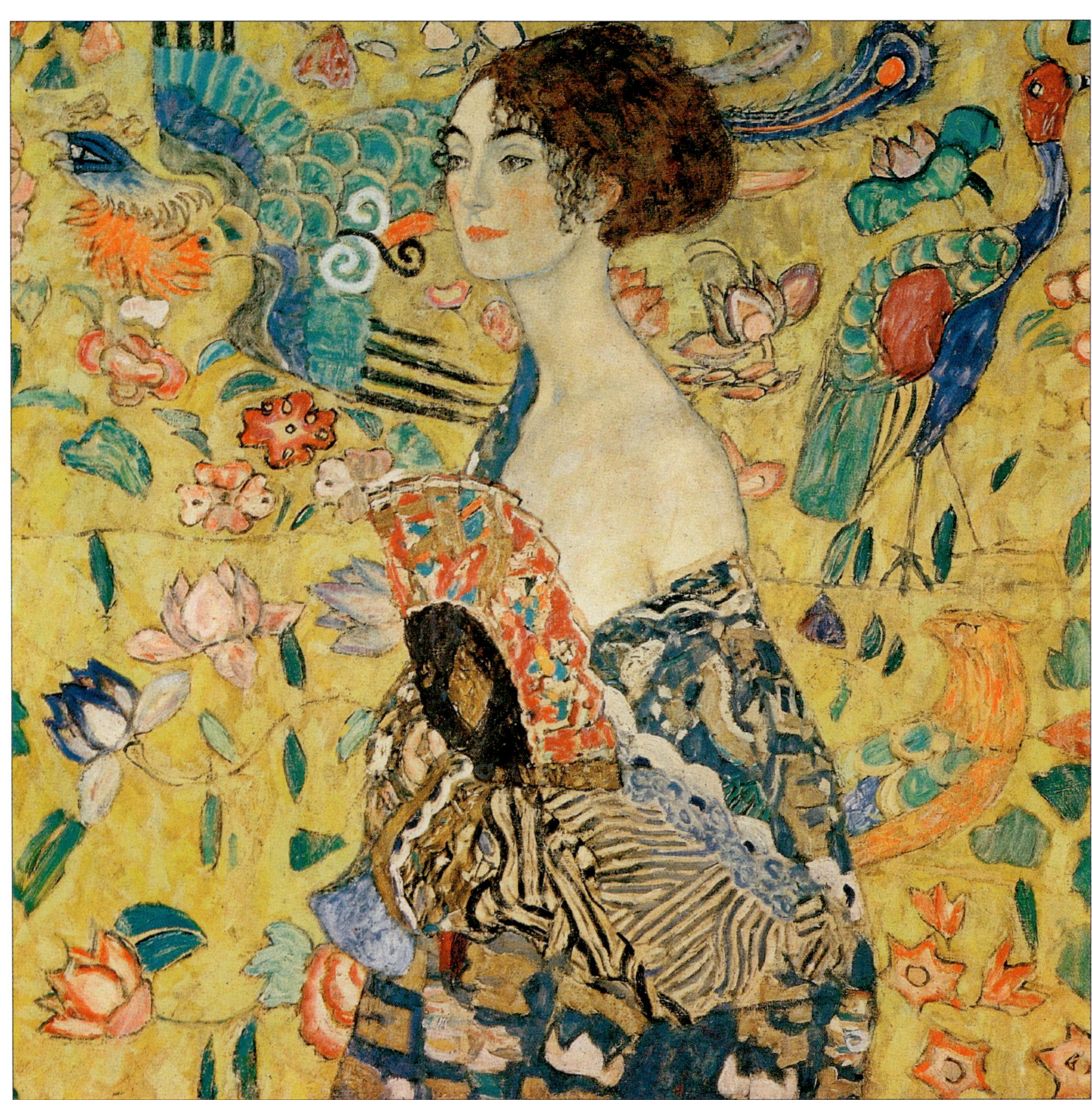

# PORTRAIT OF JOHANNA STAUDE *(Unfinished)*

*Oil on canvas. 1917–18. Österreichische Galerie, Vienna, Austria.*
*70 x 50 cm.*

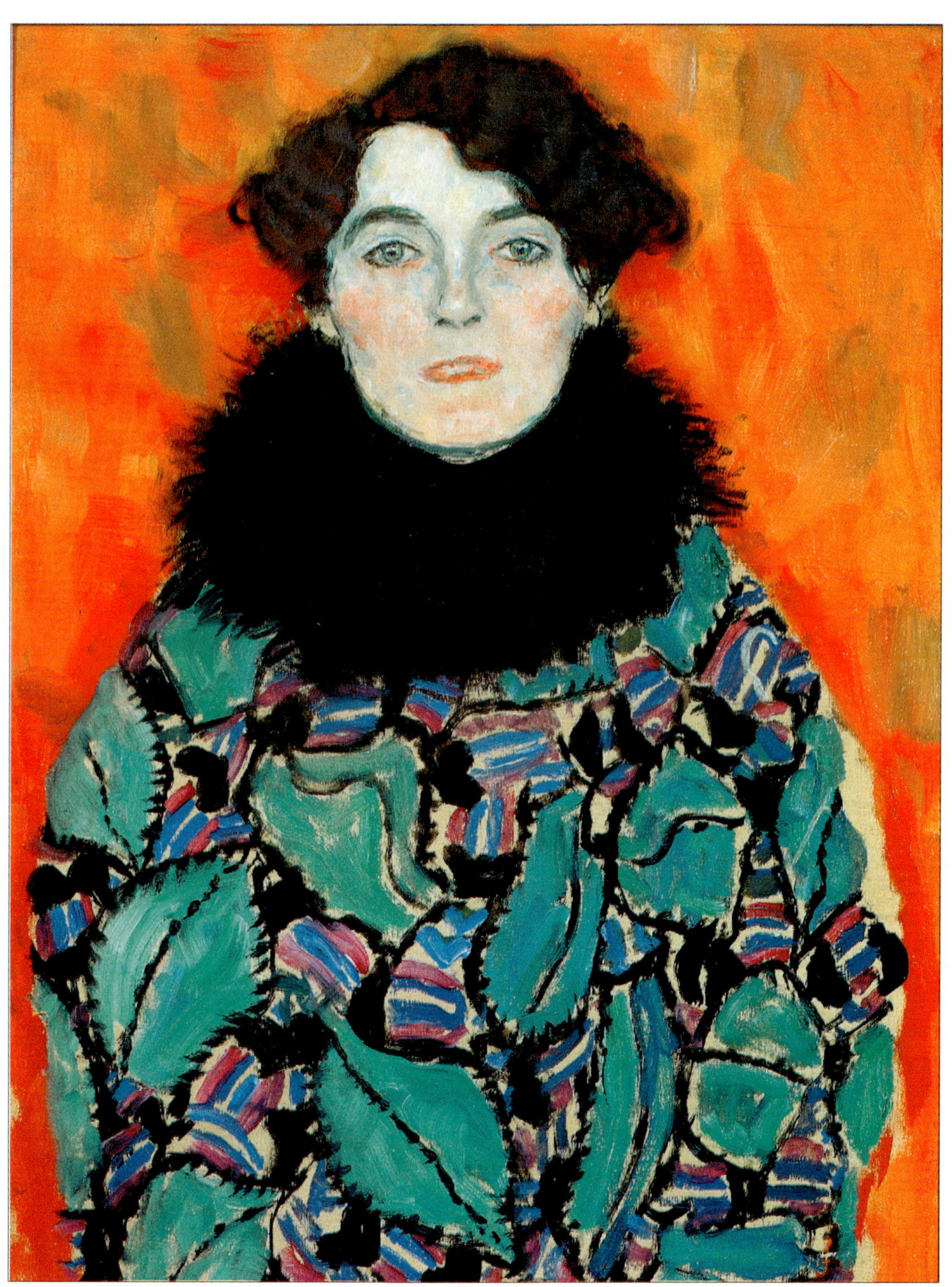

# WOMAN SEATED WITH LEGS APART

*Crayon, red chalk, and chalk on paper. 1916–17.*
*Private collection. 57 x 37.5 cm.*

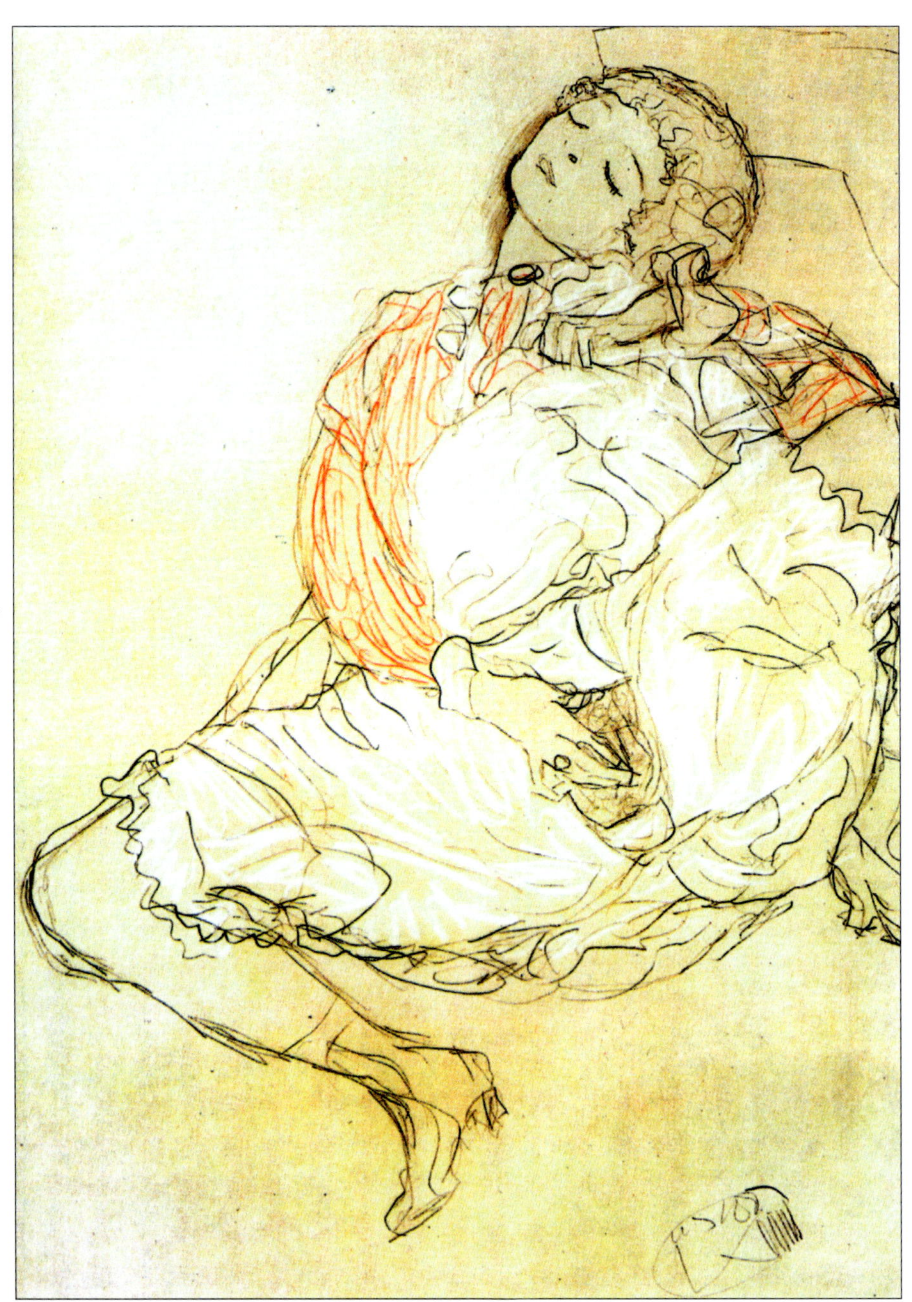

# RIE MUNK III

*Unfinished. Oil on canvas. 1917–18.*
*Neue Galerie, Linz, Austria. 180 x 90 cm.*

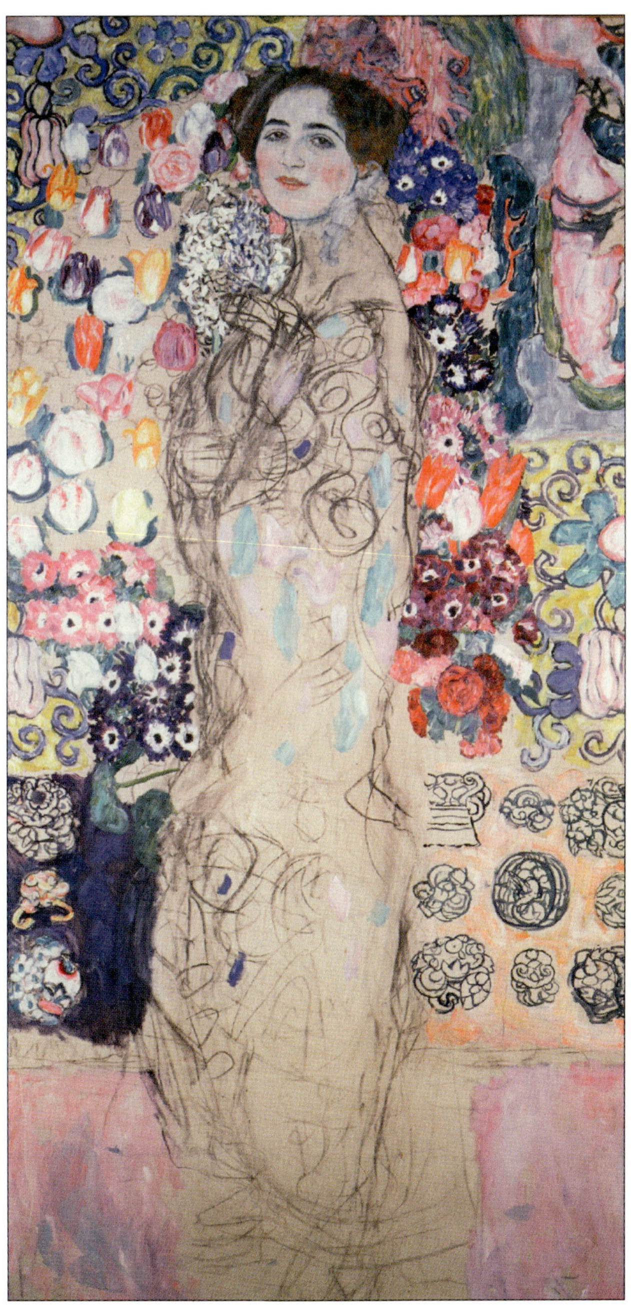

# ADAM AND EVE

*Unfinished. Oil on canvas. 1917–18.*
*Österreichische Galerie Belvedere, Vienna, Austria. 173 x 60 cm.*

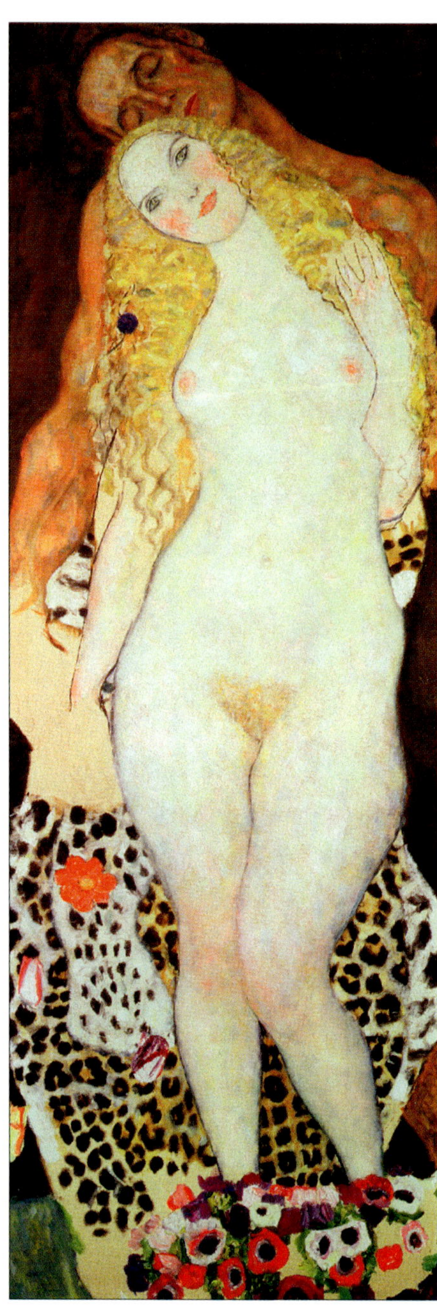

*Oil on canvas. 1917–18. Private Collection, Vienna. 166 x 190 cm.*



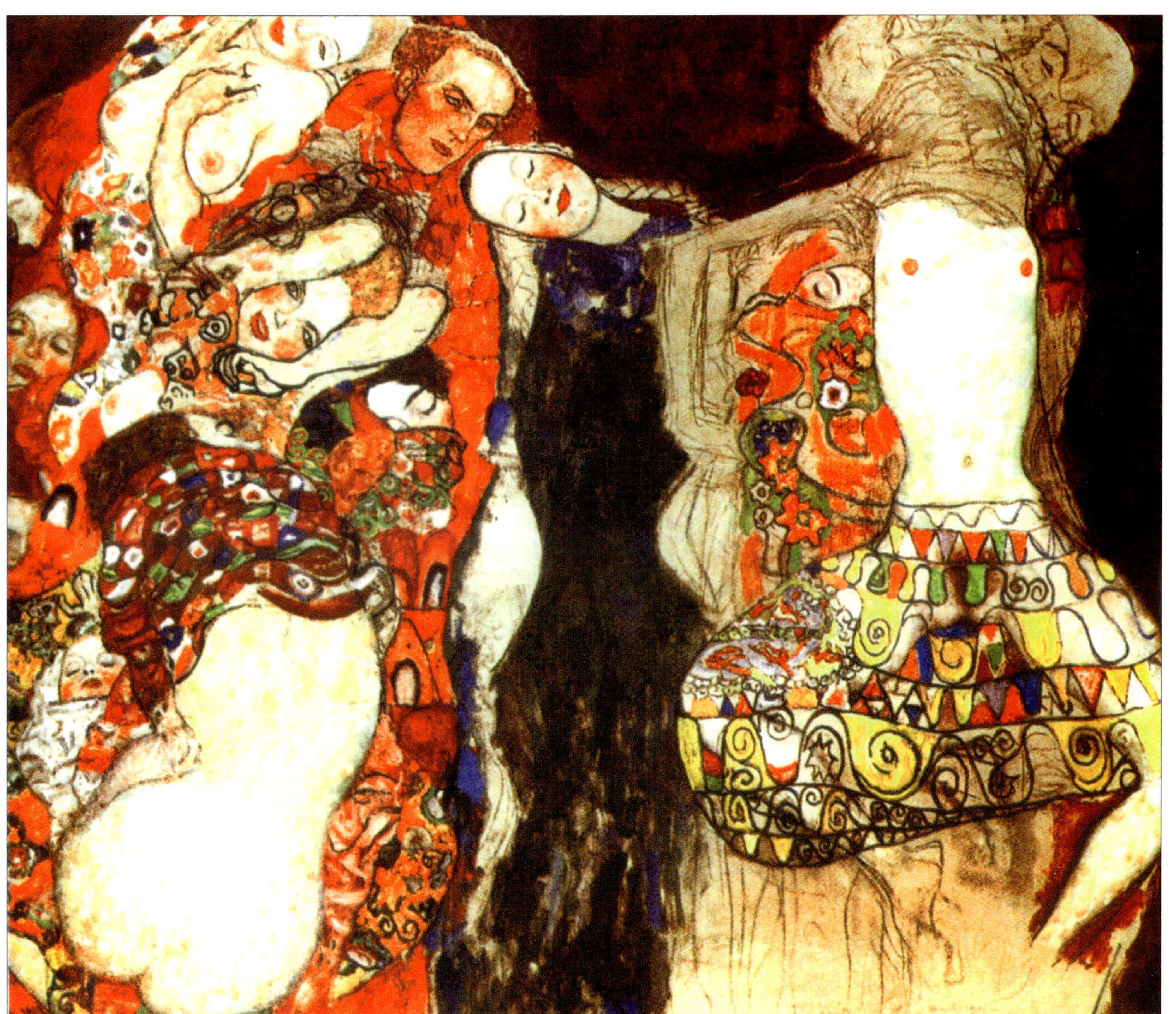